CW00859149

NOTJOHN'S GUIDE

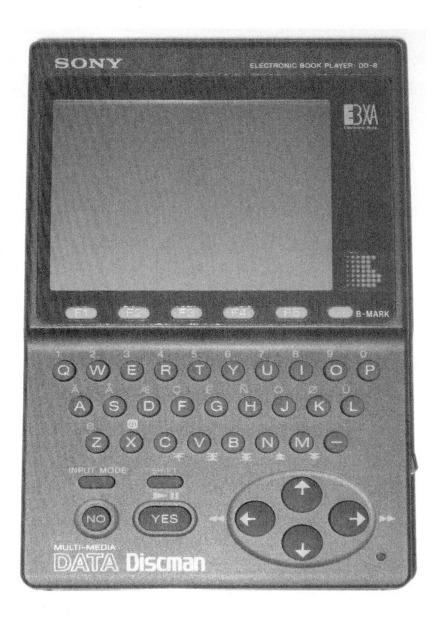

Notjohn's Guide to E-Book Formatting

Ten Steps to Getting Your Book Ready To Sell Online, Digital and Paperback (2020 Edition)

N.J. Notjohn

Enjay Press

Revised and Updated August 2020

Copyright

I hope you have learned from *Notjohn's Guide*, and I welcome your suggestions for improving it. You can email me at the Gmail address above. And I will be immensely grateful if you post a review on the online bookstore where you purchased the book. These reviews are an essential resource, and it's sad but true that readers of e-books seldom bother to post their comments, good or bad! You can also make suggestions in the course of writing a review. Believe me, I read them all. Thank you! — *N J Notjohn, August 2020*

Contents

6

Ten Steps to Digital Publishing

E-BOOKS HAVE BEEN around for a quarter of a century, but for most of that time they were the answer to a question nobody was asking. Get a load of the **Sony Data Discman** on page 2! Introduced in 1992, this "electronic book player" displayed encyclopedia essays, foreign language dictionaries, and novels from prerecorded discs. Not surprisingly, it didn't catch on outside Japan, nor did most of its successors.

Then, in 1999, came **Fatbrain**. The company had a decent business plan, selling digital editions (including several of mine) to be read on a Windows or Mac computer. Alas, Fatbrain was bought out by the Barnes & Noble bookstore company, which just didn't know what to do with it. Fatbrain withered on the vine, while B&N waited for someone else to show the way.

More promising was **Mobipocket**, a French company that developed the "mobi" format that enabled us to read e-books on a portable device, though it would be a while before Apple put a smartphone in the world's pocket. (Even better, Mobipocket also supplied "Creator" software for people like me who wanted to build e-books.) However, few people noticed Mobipocket before it was acquired by a company with deep pockets and unlimited ambition: Amazon.

Meanwhile, Japan's electronic giant launched the first **Sony Reader** in 2004, with a battery-thrifty "e-ink" screen. My daughter, who was setting off with her husband and two small children to sail around the world, bought a pair of them. A volunteer at the Gutenberg Project burned two compact discs for her, so she could take a thousand public-domain classics for the girls to read. (Those two kids have since mastered high-school biology on a ten-inch Fire tablet, and the older girl took the tablet to college last fall.)

Unlike Barnes & Noble, Amazon knew exactly what to do with its acquisition. Jeff Bezos told his boffins to mine the Mobipocket format and to build a dedicated e-book device to exploit it. The first **Kindle** made its debut on November 19, 2007, selling out in five and a half hours at $399 a copy. The market really caught fire with that first clunky device. Amazon's participation gave the digital revolution the muscle and the critical mass it needed.

Just as important, from my point of view, Amazon launched its Digital Text Platform that same month. With the DTP (now called the KDP, for Kindle Direct Publishing), authors could bypass the traditional gate-keepers — literary agents, publishers, and bookstores. (They could also, unfortunately, bypass copy editors and proof-readers, a problem that has dimmed the reputation of self-published books.) What used to take a year or two, from finishing a book to seeing it on the shelf, could now be done in a week.

I set up a Kindle account that same month, sold a few books in December, passed the $10 payout threshold in January 2008, and received my first electronic payment in March. Wow. Not only were e-books quick to publish, they were also quick to pay! Just as it once took a year or more for a book to be edited, set in type, printed, and published, so did it take at least a year for that first royalty statement to arrive (by postal mail, of course, and with a paper check). No longer! A writer-publisher can look forward to payment in less than three months, assuming he or she manages to sell a few books.

Not surprisingly, authors seized the opportunity. From 88,000 Kindle titles in November 2007, Amazon's selection has grown to *six or eight million*, with maybe a half-million more added each year. Success in this crowded market has become correspondingly hard to earn, so temper your expectations accordingly. My own sales peaked in January 2012, even though I have added a new title or two every year.

Soon there was competition, notably Barnes & Noble, Apple, and Kobo, while Sony dropped out. There are other players, too, including Google, Scribd, and Overdrive, which provides e-books to libraries. All use the now-standard and superior **epub** format. Even Amazon has adapted epub to its own requirements, though Kindle books can't be read on epub software, nor can an epub be read on a Kindle.

These competitors make up a significant market, but they are nowhere near the size of the Kindle mini-verse. American shoppers (and the US is by far the largest market for digital content) buy 70-75 percent of their e-books from Amazon, and the share is larger for self-published books. I don't think I'm unusual in finding that 80 percent of my sales come from the Amazon stores. That reflects the advertising power of the Big Five publishing companies: Penguin Random House, Simon & Schuster, HarperCollins, Macmillan, and Hachette, each with a family of imprints. Shoppers go to an online bookstore primed to buy the latest Lee Child or J K Rowling. But they find our books by looking around the store, and Amazon has the best search engine.

For a while there, my sales pattern changed back to the old 75/25 split, less because the competition strengthened than because Kindle sales faded. Paperback sales also remained strong, even on the Amazon store. The moral: don't limit yourself to a single format or a single market, even if that market is a big one. The world changes, and we don't always know why.

From Word to html to epub

I uploaded my first three or four books as **Microsoft Word** documents. They were okay, but I decided that I needed more control over how they turned out, and I switched to **html**, the "hyper-text markup language" used to build web pages. Despite its rather terrifying name (why hyper? why text? why markup? and above all, why *language?*), html is just a simple way of tagging text so that a web page looks as you want it to look when seen on a computer monitor. Most tags come in pairs, one for starting an action, the other for ending it. For example —

<b>Let's make this sentence boldface</b>

— appears on the computer or e-reader or smartphone as **Let's make this sentence boldface**. What could be simpler and less terrifying?

Now here's a secret that many author-publishers would rather not hear: *An e-book is just a web page, written in html. And a dedicated e-reader (or an "app" that you install on your computer, tablet, or smartphone) is just a special-purpose web browser*. When you upload a Word doc to the KDP, or let Word save your document as html, you're letting Microsoft format your book. And guess what? Sometimes the software does an acceptable job, but sometimes it fails miserably. That's because even the most innocent-looking Word doc can contain all sorts of formatting horrors behind the pretty facade. Word does a good job of hiding bad formatting, but the errors can show up in the Kindle or other device and in the "Look Inside" sample on the store page. Can you think of any worse place for bad formatting than on the free sample that any intelligent customer is going to look at before pressing the Buy Now button?

So from 2009 through 2011, I wrote my own html

documents and uploaded them to the Kindle platform. This worked beautifully, though it was a clunky process, especially when there were illustrations in the book. And the zip file didn't work on Barnes & Noble and the other booksellers, all of whom had settled upon the rival, open-source **epub format** for their books.

Then, in January 2012, a gracious formatter let me in on a secret: epubs translate just fine on the Kindle platform. Wow! Do you realize how huge that is? *I needed only the one document to sell my book through any retailer*, from Amazon to Barnes & Noble to Apple to Walmart. (I do make one small alteration, to get past a potential problem on the KDP platform: I remove the included cover in the version that goes to Amazon. Otherwise there's a risk that the Kindle version will display two covers, one after the other.)

So I learned to make epubs. All my recent books, and most of those I published earlier, are in this format. I cannot recommend it too highly. If you can write a book in Word, you can transform it into an epub, and it won't cost you a penny. This guidebook will show you how. It's set up like a cookbook or a military training manual, breaking the publishing process down into bite-sized steps. (Did you know that you can learn to ski by the numbers? That's how the US Army does it!) Just follow the cookbook, and the end product will be a handsome e-book on Amazon's worldwide stores, and on those of Apple, Barnes & Noble, Walmart, Google Play, and perhaps your local library.

Now, I don't actually follow those ten steps myself. I go straight from Word to html to epub. But I think it's essential that you know how to build a title page, a table of contents, the copyright page, and all that other stuff before you start taking shortcuts. As you read along with me, however, you'll soon realize that these tasks can easily be streamlined if you equip yourself with a few powerful — and free! — programs, the most important of which is **Sigil**.

Plan B

And if after reading the following chapters you still find the process daunting, I also provide Plan B: The Ultimate Basic Template (page 90). With a bit of tweaking, and with no real knowledge of html, you can fit a novel or a simple non-fiction book into this framework. The result is an html file that is readily accepted by Kindle Direct Publishing (though not, alas, by most of the other online stores). With that glorious moment behind you, I trust that you will come back and give the Ten-Step Epub another chance to serve your needs.

Fixed format books

Most e-books are **reflowable**. Unless you have locked it in place, you can hold your e-reader vertically, in *portrait* mode, or you can turn it sideways for the *landscape* view. The text will flow to fit the width of the screen, and if you choose a larger or smaller typeface, that too will change the flow. In the early years, all e-books worked this way. Alas, it doesn't work very well with picture books, textbooks, and children's books, so companies introduced **fixed format** to mimic the appearance of a print edition.

I stay away from fixed format for two reasons. First, the systems are proprietary: if you build your e-book to Apple's standards, you can't upload it to Kindle Direct Publishing, and if you follow an Amazon template, it won't be accepted by Apple. (And neither will work at Barnes & Noble.) Worse, even if you're content to remain within the Kindle mini-verse, your fixed format book can only be viewed on a Kindle Fire or other tablet, not on one of the tens of millions of e-ink Kindles. As for smartphones, forget it! How does one read a biology text or a graphic novel on a four-inch screen?

And fixed format books are usually much more bulky than reflowable ones — thousands of megabytes — so download fees will eat up part of your profit on the Amazon store. For all these reasons, I have nothing to say about fixed format e-books in the following chapters.

Before you go any further...

What I'm about to say shouldn't be necessary, but I'm going to say it anyway: *Buy a Kindle.* At this writing, I see one as cheap as $69.99 on the US Amazon store. Better yet, buy a Kindle, a Fire tablet (starting at $49.99), and perhaps a Nook and a Kobo Reader, though those are pricier and the payoff likely to be smaller.

Then buy or borrow an iPad, so you can see what Apple does to your books. Finally, download every possible app for all the electronic devices you own.

Once you have equipped yourself, please take another step before you presume to publish your first e-book. Go to the Amazon store that serves your country (it may well be the US store) and download the free samples of the top ten or twenty best-sellers. If you write genre fiction or specialized stuff, also download samples of your competitors' work, especially those published by the Big Five houses. Read them. *Study them.* Please!

And while you're at it, take down the first ten or twenty books from your bookshelf and study *them.* (You're a writer, so you do have a bookshelf, right?) You would be astonished, as I regularly am, at how many authors set out to become publishers without having a clue about how books are designed and formatted. In a later chapter, I will recommend **The Chicago Manual of Style**, which has an excellent chapter on book-making. There are also good resources online. Read about books and e-books; study the most successful examples; and adopt the best practices as your own.

Step 1 - Your Html Template

FIRST GET RID of the notion that html is "code." It's just a way of tagging words, paragraphs, and chapter heads so they show up on a screen as they would on paper. A document thus tagged is inserted into a framework that tells the computer (and all e-book devices are little computers, just as all digital books are html files) that this is indeed html, or xml or xhtml, to name a few variations. My framework (call it a template, if you must, though it's really not that) is shown below, and to make matters easier I've posted it on my blog so you can copy it and paste it into your plain-text or html software. The same is true of the style sheet recommended in the chapter that follows.

But about that text editor: *don't use Microsoft Word* or any word processor for this task. In the early years, most of the horror stories on the Kindle author forums resulted from using Word for creating html. The problem is what you *don't* see. Word itself is an html program, and behind the scenes it's littering your book with instructions that are invisible to you but will be seen and obeyed by the html conversion and eventually by the Kindle device or app that people use to read your book. There's a much better way of going about it. We will get to that shortly.

The same formatter who turned me on to epub is much kinder about Word than I am. But she is a professional who has formatted thousands of e-books, and she knows how to make software sing — and I'm sure she has never actually uploaded a Word doc to the KDP.

If you are determined to use Word, the secret is to be

obsessive about employing heading and paragraph Styles, rather than treating it like a typewriter. If you want to give Styles a try, check Notjohn's Blog for some pointers. Especially read "All about e-publishing," which at this writing is fourth from the top.

For now, all you need to know is that the following lines of html will provide the necessary scaffolding or framework for your book. You will copy it to clipboard, paste it into a text editor, then add the elements of your book. The result will be a simple-minded document and one that actually wouldn't pass an html validation. That doesn't matter because you are going to go directly from html to epub, and trust me: the epub will be okay.

The framework

```
<?xml version="1.0" encoding="utf-8"?>
<!DOCTYPE html PUBLIC "-//W3C//DTD XHTML 1.1//EN"
 "http://www.w3.org/TR/xhtml11/DTD/xhtml11.dtd">
<html xmlns="http://www.w3.org/1999/xhtml">

<head>
<title>Your Book Title Goes Here</title>
<link rel="stylesheet" type="text/css" href="epub.css">
</head>

<body>
<!--Your title page goes here-->
<!--Then your table of contents-->
<!--And your book file-->
<!--And finally, your copyright and author pages-->
```

```
</body>
</html>
```

The framework is divided into three parts. The first consists of four lines of boilerplate that you should just take on faith. Next comes the **head**, which contains only one piece of information that matters: you should replace **Your Book Title Goes Here** with ... the title of your book! It is followed by a pointer to the style sheet (epub.css) that will tell the digital reader how to display your book. (You could paste the entire style sheet in the heading, but having it as a separate file will cut down on the size of your finished book.) Finally, for the **body** of the book, I show several **comments** to suggest the book elements you probably will want to add. You can delete each comment as you add a section, or you can leave it in place. "Commented" material isn't visible in the book as you view it in a Kindle or other e-reader.

Finally, there are closing tags to end the body section and also the html document as a whole. In most cases, every html tag is matched by a closing tag, something that is too often neglected when you use an automatic conversion to turn your book into an html file.

Enough said! You can duplicate the framework, or you can go to Notjohn's Guide on Blogspot and copy it to clipboard. Then paste it into any plain-text editor such as **Notepad** that comes with every Windows computer. If you use Notepad for this purpose, it will save your book file with a **txt** extension instead of the **htm** or **html** extension that is called for. You can use the "all files" option instead and type the extension yourself, or you can change the extension later.

Notepad++ and NoteTab

There are two alternatives to the simple text editor. To

start, you might try the free and excellent **Notepad++**, which is easy to use and handles html very prettily. Find the website, go to Download, find the most recent release, and choose the Installer for your Windows computer, probably the one for a 64-bit machine.

If you are serious about working with html, and can handle a steeper learning curve, **NoteTab** is a great text editor and html tool. The full-featured version is Note-Tab 7, which costs $40. You can also get a 30-day trial, and there's also a freeware Light version that will handle most e-book formatting chores.

You may find Notepad++ more user-friendly. Html tags are shown in color, and if you forget to close a tag it will show up in purple. Note that when saving an html file, you should select the **Encoding** option as **Encode in UTF-8**, which can handle other alphabets and symbols, such as the French acute or German umlaut. The default encoding of "ANSI" is intended for the English language. (And you have declared your allegiance to utf-8, in the very first line of the framework.)

There's no Mac version of these programs, but **Barebones Software** has an editor called BBEdit that has been recommended to me. It's free to download and to use, but a $50 license gives you access to many advanced features after the 30-day evaluation period.

I must make a confession here: In this chapter and the ones immediately following, I'm asking you to follow the same painful process I used in the early years of self-publishing. In a later chapter I will introduce you to the magnificent **Sigil** software, which will do much of the routine work for you. (When you open a new epub, for example, the basic head-and-body framework is already there.) But you can't use Sigil without a working knowledge of html. Trust me: it's worth knowing this stuff.

Step 2 - Your Style Sheet

PEOPLE WHO PLAY with computers have a habit of inventing names that baffle the rest of us. Thus the Cascading Style Sheet or **CSS** that tells the digital device how to display text, headings, images, and the like. For our purpose, nothing cascades, so we will simply call it a "style sheet." It's a file that will be read by the **Sigil** software you'll use to finish your book.

I built my style sheet through trial and error, so it's meant to handle situations that are common to me. You will find it at Notjohn's KDP Guide on Blogspot. You prob-ably won't use all these styles, and you may not use most of them. But there is nothing to be lost by including them in your style sheet. Who knows? They may come in handy in the future.

You'll recall that one line in the <head> section of the framework reads like this:

<link rel="stylesheet" type="text/css" href="epub.css">

It points to a style sheet named **epub.css**. My model style sheet is fairly complicated, so you should go to my blog and copy it entire. Paste it into your text editor (NotePad, NoteTab, whatever) and save it with the file name of *epub*. In time you will change that to *epub.css* so Sigil can find it when you are finishing your book. The style sheet provides:

Four paragraph 'classes'

The style sheet begins with a basic paragraph class or

style that, with a few exceptions, will be used all through your book:

```
p {
margin-top:0.0em;
margin-bottom:0.0em;
text-indent:1.5em;
text-align:justify;
}
```

To break that down, any paragraph beginning **<p>** will have no extra space above or below it (zero **margin-top** and **margin-bottom**). The first line will be indented about four letters (**text-indent**), while the rest of the text will be **justified** or carried out flush to the left and right margins (**text-align:justify**), as in a printed book. If you like, you can call for **text-align:left**, but I don't recommend it. How many books in your library are formatted "ragged right"?

Next we have three special-purpose paragraph classes:

```
p.first {
margin-top:0.5em;
margin-bottom: 0.0em;
text-indent:0.0em;
text-align:justify;
}

p.left {
margin-top:0.5em;
margin-bottom: 0.0em;
text-indent:0.0em;
text-align:left;
}

p.center {
margin-top:0.0em;
margin-bottom:0.25em;
```

```
text-indent:0.0em;
text-align:center;
}
```

I use the **p.first** class for any paragraph that begins a chapter, major section, or significant change of thought or scene. (This is just such a paragraph.) There is no indent, and a there's a bit of extra space between it and whatever precedes it. And the text is justified. Wherever you want such a paragraph to appear, you begin it with **<p class="first">**.

Next comes **p.left**, for a left-aligned paragraph. I created this for quotations and suchlike bits of prose that are to be set off from the regular flow of text. (I don't use it much any more, relying instead on italics to do the job.) Finally, there's a paragraph style called **p.center**, for whenever I want to center a line or two. (In my table of contents, for example.) Again, these paragraphs start with **<p class="left">** or **<p class="center">**.

With rare exceptions, every opening tag must be matched with a closing tag, identified by a slash. So every paragraph in your book should end with a **</p>**. Amazon's valuable **Look Inside!** sample is especially vulnerable to the damage done by unclosed tags.

Chapter titles and sub-heads

Now we turn to the **headings** that will break your book into chapters and sections. The style sheet provides three possibilities, from the hefty one that I use for chapter heads, down to a small "breakhead" that's basically just a bolded statement that sits flush left. ("Chapter titles and sub-heads" above is just such a breakhead.)

```
h2 {
margin-top:1em;
```

```
font-size: 150%;
text-indent: 0em;
font-style: italic;
text-align:center;
}
h3 {
margin-top:1em;
font-size: 125%;
text-indent: 0em;
text-align:center;
}
h4 {
margin-top:1em;
font-size: 125%;
text-indent: 0em;
text-align:left;
}
```

These headings, from **<h2>** to **<h4>**, make up what the boffins call a "hierarchy." That is, they tell your web browser (or your e-book device) how they relate to one another, from most important to least important. So when you open an html file in Sigil, the software will sort the headings for the table of contents, and also of course determine how large it is and whether it is centered or flush left. More about the table of contents in Step 3, and more about headings in Step 6.

And of course every heading must have a closing tag, from **</h2>** to **</h4>**.

Building your title page

You'll notice that there's no **<h1>** tag in my style sheet. That's because I started out by using <h1> for the title of the book on my title page, with <h2> for the subtitle, and

<h4> for the author and publisher. I had my knuckles rapped for what the boffins regard as *bad code,* and I stopped the practice, which gave me no further use for the <h1> tag. Instead, I built a set of paragraph styles just for the title page, and for other uses in the book that have nothing to do with chapter headings and breaks, so as to keep them out of the table of contents. They are the next three styles in my CSS:

```
p.large {
font-weight: bold;
margin-top:1em;
margin-bottom:1em;
font-size: 200%;
text-indent: 0em;
font-style: italic;
text-align:center;
}

p.medium {
margin-top:1em;
margin-bottom:1em;
font-weight: bold;
font-size: 150%;
margin-top:1.0em;
text-indent: 0em;
font-style: italic;
text-align:center;
}

p.small {
font-weight: bold;
margin-bottom:1em;
font-size: 125%;
text-indent: 0em;
text-align:center;
}
```

I used **p.large** for the book's title, **p.medium** for the subtitle, and **p.small** for the author's name and that of the publisher. They're centered horizontally on the page, and they provide a refreshing bit of space between the three levels. They work well on all e-book reading experiences, from a computer screen through the various dedicated devices down to my obsolescent iPhone 4. Since these are paragraphs, not headings, you must specify a class for each, such as **<p class="large">** or **<p class="medium">**, etc., and end with **</p>**.

Note that **p.medium** will appear on the page as the exact equivalent of an <h2> heading, except that it won't be picked up for the table of contents. Similarly, **p.small** will look just like an <h3> heading and can be used in place of it if you don't want the software to include it in the table of contents.

I have since adopted another way to build a title page, which I'll discuss in Step 3. For this Guide, however, I continued to use these paragraph classes, so you can turn to my title page and see them in action.

Blockquotes

Next, the style sheet provides two paragraph classes that you can use to set off text in dramatic fashion:

```
p.block {
font-family: courier, monospace;
font-weight: bold;
text-indent: 1em;
text-align:left;
margin:0em 0em 0em 1em;
}
p.blockcenter {
font-family: courier, monospace;
```

```
font-weight: bold;
text-align:center;
margin:0em 0em 0em 1em;
}
```

I use **p.block** for paragraphs that I really want to distinguish from the rest of the text, for example if I'm quoting a newspaper or a typescript. The typeface is **Courier**, which looks like typewritten text. (All style sheet elements shown on these pages are set in just this typeface.) Next is a very similar paragraph class called **p.blockcenter**, for when you want to display something (a newspaper headline, for example) centered on the page. As with the other paragraph classes, they start with **<p class="block">** or **<p class="blockcenter">** and end with **</p>**).

In both those classes, I have added the instruction **font-weight: bold;** so they'll show up better in the published book. The Courier typeface is unfortunately very light.

Small caps

During the last century, publishers developed a tradition of opening each chapter with a "drop cap" — an over-sized letter, sometimes very fancy, and extending two or three lines into the text. I am a strong believer in making my e-books look as much like print editions as possible, but drop caps are tricky. They can be accomplished, but not in every case and not on every device. I gave up using them a few years ago, when Amazon arbitrarily changed the line spacing in Kindle books, with the result that all my lovely drop caps suddenly looked stupid.

I continue to use drop caps in print editions, but for e-books I now put the first few words of each chapter's opening paragraph in capital letters, slightly smaller than the text, and presented in boldface type. Here is the style:

```
span.smallcap {
font-size: 90%;
font-weight: bold;
}
```

Note that this is a **span**, not a paragraph class. A span affects one or more words within the paragraph. Thus, in the digital edition, the opening phrase in this chapter was marked up like this:

```
<p class="first"><span class="smallcap">
PEOPLE WHO PLAY </span>
```

Some older devices (including the first two generations of Kindle, plus the Kindle DX that was sold as recently as 2014) won't obey the 90 percent instruction. No matter. The opening still looks good at 100 percent.

I think this is worth doing — but it is, after all, a *decoration*. If you're going to ignore anything in this book, let it be this section.

Images and captions

The final three classes are to take care of images in your book.

```
div.image {
text-align:center;
margin-bottom: 0.25em;
}

div.icon {
text-align:center;
margin-bottom: 1em;
}
```

```
div.caption {
margin-top: .25em;
margin-bottom: 1em;
text-align:center;
font-style:italic;
}
```

The first is a division called **div.image**, which centers an image horizontally on the page. The same is true of **div.icon**, which I use for my publisher icon on the title page. (It sits between the author name and that of the publishing house, and is also called a **colophon**. There's a bit of extra space between it and the line above.) You may find other uses for it as well.

Finally, there is **div.caption**, a style for the short description beneath an illustration. It will be centered horizontally on the page, in italics, with a bit of space between the caption and the image above it. I generally shy away from captions in e-books, preferring to work the information into the preceding paragraph.

Like the various paragraph styles, divisions are called up by the instructions **<div class="image">**, **<div class="icon">**, or **<div class="caption">**. And of course you will close the division with the tag **</div>**.

Working with Styles

These styles or classes are arranged in no particular order, and there is nothing sacred about their names. I built my style sheet over several years, as I learned more and more about styling an e-book, which mostly explains the order of their arrangement and the names I gave to them. You can rearrange them to suit your way of working, or give them names that make more sense to you.

An important point about type size: an e-book can be and probably will be read on a variety of gadgets, from a 21-inch computer screen to a 4-inch smartphone. (I still read books on my venerable iPhone 4, when I'm traveling or waiting for the show to begin.) For that reason, it's a bad idea to call for exact sizes, such as the one-third-inch (or one-centimeter) indent commonly used in Microsoft Word. Instead, I specify an indent of **1.5 em**, with an "em" being the width of an upper-case (capital letter) M. (The relationship of *em* and *M* was true, at least, in the days when words were cast in hot lead on a Linotype machine. More recently, an em is considered to be equal to the height of one line of type. The difference is trivial.) By using relative measures, the indent will be less when the typeface is small and more when it is large, so it will always look right.

For the same reason, my headings are sized by a percentage figure, with the <h2> chapter titles being 150 percent, or half again as large as the text of the book. When you start to work with print editions, you will become familiar with **points**, which are used to indicate the size of type on the page. There are 72 points to an inch. A common size for text is 12 points, so with that as a guide, you can figure that you are using 18-point type for the chapter heading. That doesn't sound like much, but it looks good on the e-book "page."

Your book's folder

I suggest that you save your **epub.css** file into a distinct folder with an appropriate title, so you can easily find it next day or next year. Your framework should also be there, along with any images you intend to incorporate into the book.

Again, I should emphasize that these are the beginner

steps, the ones I went through as I learned to format e-books over a period of years. I now skip most of them, going from **Word document** to **clean html** to tweaking the html in **Sigil**. Very likely you'll soon find yourself skipping steps or combining them. But it's a good idea to practice the exact recipe for *Crème au beurre classique* a few times, until you get the hang of it, before venturing to play Julia Child in front of your guests.

Step 3 - Your Title Page

YOUR TITLE PAGE should be uncluttered, simple, and fairly compact. This helps ensure that it looks good on a smartphone, a dedicated e-book device, and on a computer monitor. That's why I call for a **top margin** of 1 em for each element. It provides a bit of breathing room, without pushing the publisher's name onto another page — always a risk when the book is opened on a smartphone. (There's another and perhaps better way to accomplish this, by building your title page as an image. I'll get to that at the end of this chapter.)

Here is the html that produced the title page for this Guide:

<p class="large">Notjohn&rsquo;s Guide to E-Book Formatting</p>
<p class="medium">Ten Steps to Getting Your Book Ready to Sell Online, Digital and Paperback</p>
<p class="small">N.J. Notjohn</p>
<div class="icon"><img src="../Images/openbook.gif" width="15%" alt="Enjay Press"></a></div>
<p class="small">Enjay Press</p>
<p class="small">Revised and Updated 2020</p>

This is all pretty straightforward, with a large typeface for the title, medium for the subtitle, and small for the author, publisher, and edition information. However, there are a couple of elements that may seem strange to you.

To start with, there's an apostrophe in the first word of the title, for which I have substituted the html "entity" for a right-facing single quote, written **’**. This is a case, I'm sorry to say, where the html boffins live in a world of their own. They believe that an apostrophe must be straight, not curly, but they're wrong, at least when it comes to publishing in the English language. I know of no serious reference, whether it be *The Chicago Manual of Style*, the *Oxford English Dictionary*, or the Practical Typography website, that agrees with them. Happily, neither does Word or OpenOffice — or Google Docs, for that matter. If you write your book in any of these word processors, curly quotes and apostrophes should be the default. (If not, look for the "smart quotes" option.) They will convert nicely to html, if you follow one of the short-cuts I suggest in Step 5.

A second feature that might seem a bit odd is the call for the **icon** or "colophon" for Enjay Press, a small image that I created just for this book. If you don't want a pub-lisher symbol, just delete this division, which is structured like this:

The division has the class name **icon**, followed by **img src**= and the name of the image file, which in this case is **openbook.gif**. I found an image of an open book on the internet that was not copyrighted. I used photo editing software to impose **NJ** onto it, then I saved it as a gif file. I specified the width so that it would not be enlarged on most e-book devices. (Some older devices won't follow this instruction, but we can't please every-one. To prevent my colophon from looking gigantic on the earlier Kindles, I reduced the size of the gif file to 100x100 pixels.)

Finally, I give the **alt**= title of the image. This is a courtesy for sight-impaired readers who are using the read-aloud feature found on the better e-book devices. In this case, the read-aloud voice will pronounce my name, then "Image of book," and finally "Enjay Press."

To make life easier, I have put the basic title-page html on Notjohn's KDP Guide on Blogspot, so you can copy it and paste it to a file for future use. (Put it in the same folder as the framework saved earlier.) I have omitted the **icon** division because you may not want to use that embellishment on your first venture into digital publishing. When you are ready, just come back to this chapter and adapt the division style for your use.

A word about capitalization

I've seen a lot of e-books with the title ALL IN CAPITAL LETTERS, and others with a subtitle that has no capital letters at all. (I'm talking now about the titles as shown on Amazon's or Apple's online store, not how they look on the title page.) Both look amateurish, in my opinion, and either can cause your book to be refused by Apple, meaning that you are shut out of a fairly significant market. Later I will have occasion to recommend that you buy and study *The Chicago Manual of Style*, which explains the rules in admirable detail. But if they're too much to absorb, you won't go far wrong by obeying Apple's website, which says: *"The first letter in all words in the title and subtitle should be capitalized, except for the following words: **a, an, and, for, from, or, the, to**."* To which I hasten to add: you must also capitalize the first letter of the title and subtitle, even if the word is on Apple's list.

And Mrs. Zulauf, my twelfth-grade English teacher, would also point out that the list should have other words on it. E M Forster's novel is *A Room with a View*, not *A Room With a View*. That's why a good editor will refer to the *Chicago Manual* from time to time.

Adding your title page to the framework

You now have two text files in your book folder, a framework and a title page. Open the framework and paste the title page as the first item following the **body** tag. You can now remove the line that says **<!-- Insert your title page here -->**, though you don't *have* to do this. The exclamation mark and double hyphens indicate that it is a *comment*, not to be displayed in the final book.

Again, I should say that I no longer build an e-book this way. Instead, I finalize the text in Microsoft Word, run the Word doc through a cleanup process, and save it as an html file. I open the html file in Sigil, and only then break the book into its constituent parts. But I have been writing web pages and e-books for a good many years. Unless you're handy with html, you should take these steps one at a time until you understand how it all works.

A way around all that

A few years ago, I noticed that the Big Five publishers and even some smaller ones were taking a new approach to the title page: they simply reproduced the title page of the print edition. That provides more continuity between the two editions, plus it eliminates a bit of formatting. I thought it was such a great idea that I have adopted it for any book that has a print edition, and more recently for some that don't. I just mock up a good-looking page in Microsoft Word and take a screenshot of it. (I use the freeware version of Gadwin PrintScreen for this purpose.)

To include an image rather than a page of html, you'll use the **div.image** class and add a **width="100%"** instruction, as explained in Step 8. Here for example is the html for the illustration on the following page, showing where the width instruction was inserted:

<div class="image"> <img alt="Contents page" src="../Images/contentspage.gif" width="100%"/> </div>

Which is probably more than you wanted to know at this point. Don't worry about it; just take it one step at a time.

Step 4 - Your Contents Page

AND NOW FOR your Table of Contents, or TOC as it is called in the publishing biz. I have posted a simple TOC framework on Notjohn's KDP Guide on Blogspot that will be recognized by the Kindle's "Go To" function. Wherever a reader may be in the book, he or she can use that function to bring up the actual (html) TOC in the front of the book. (I put it just after the title page.) Note that I use the single word **Contents** to head up the list. That seems sufficient to me — it's not really a *table*, after all.

The chapter titles are in the form of hyperlinks or "hotlinks" like those used on the web. I like to give my chapters sexy titles, because the TOC as seen in the online sample at some stores is a brilliant sales tool, informing the reader about the content to follow and hopefully leaving him or her eager to read it. (Amazon, alas, now forces many but not all e-books to open at page one, chapter one. This reduces the value of the TOC, since few shoppers will bother to page back to the front matter. Some of the competing online stores either don't show a preview or make it hard to find.)

For purposes of my framework, I just title them Chapter One, Chapter Two, and so on; I trust you will be more imaginative. I stop with Chapter Five because that will give you the general idea (just use copy-and-paste to add as many chapters as you like), and I conclude with a link to the **Copyright Page** and **About the Author**. In printed books, the copyright information usually follows the title page, but in an e-book it might as well go at the end.

The basic Contents page

```
<h2 id="toc">Contents</h2>
<p class="center"><a
href="#chapter01">Chapter One</a></p>
<p class="center"><a
href="#chapter02">Chapter Two</a></p>
<p class="center"><a
href="#chapter03">Chapter Three</a></p>
<p class="center"><a
href="#chapter04">Chapter Four</a></p>
<p class="center"><a
href="#chapter05">Chapter Five</a></p>
<p class="center"><a href="#copy">Copyright
- About the Author</a></p>
```

Again, you can copy this framework from my blog, paste it into your text editor, and adapt it to your book.

Note that each hotlink contains a statement such as **a href="#chapter01"** which tells the software to look for a chapter heading with the identifier **id="chapter01"**. The combination is what makes the hotlink hot. You can of course call your chapters with named identifiers, as I have done with **a href="copy"** for the Copyright Page. There are advantages to both systems.

Don't worry now about placing the identifiers within the chapter headings themselves. We'll get to that later. For now it is sufficient to build your table of contents in a text editor (Notepad will do; Notepad++ is better, and some of us think that NoteTab is best of all) and to paste it into the appropriate place in your html framework.

Later we will meet the excellent (and free) **Sigil** software, which will actually build an html TOC for you, based on your heading styles. More important, the software will also build the "logical" table of contents now required for e-books, a process so daunting that I hold my breath with admiration for any self-publisher who attempts it.

Sigil is designed to split your book into multiple sections, as is standard for epub editions. The older devices tended to choke on long files, and even the newer ones work faster if they don't have to load an entire book each time you open it. Conveniently for the author-publisher, the act of splitting the book in Sigil will actually build the chapter links for you, so you may find with experience that you can streamline this process. I am inclined to do it the old-fashioned way, because I built my books with html before I discovered this remarkable piece of software. And, as always, I think it's a good idea to understand how the engine works before you set out to build an automobile.

Step 5 - From Document to Html

PROBABLY YOU WROTE your book in Microsoft Word, the most popular word processor in the world. Its major competitors are **WordPerfect** from Corel Software and the free and excellent (and very similar) **OpenOffice** and **LibreOffice** suites. For computers running Apple software, there is **Pages**. Finally, there's **Google Docs**, a free online word processor from the internet giant. The least desirable of these programs, for building an e-book, seems to be WordPerfect. Recent versions of Pages also seem to be problematic. Google Docs has a reputation for producing messy html, as does the **InDesign** software often used by professional book designers. I hasten to add that each of these programs has its fans — and, as is often the case with those who hold a minority position, they can be vociferous in defending it.

Probably you asked Word or its alternative to convert "straight quotes" to "curly quotes," and double hyphens (-- to fully formed em dashes (—). Though not strictly necessary, these touches will make your book look more like one from a New York publisher instead of a high-school book report. If you haven't done so already, I suggest that you do this before you save your book file for conversion.

And here is something else you might do, to make life easier as you build your first epub: Go through your file and insert a double asterisk (**) in front of every chapter title and other heading or sub-head. This will enable you to find them quickly and put them in final form as shown in Step 6.

Versions of Word from 1997 to 2003 saved files in a format with the extension ***.doc**, which soon became the more or less universal format. Later versions of Word, beginning with 2007, default to the ***.docx** version, which has become the new standard. (In the cunning way of software geeks, the *X* stands for Extensible Markup Language or XML.) As the end user, formatting a book that will uploaded as an epub, it scarcely matters whether you work in *.doc or in *docx.

You may well encounter problems, however, if you use WordPerfect, Google Docs, or Pages, especially the newer versions of Pages. If you favor an Apple computer, or if you can't afford or aren't willing to pay for Microsoft Word, my advice is to download and use OpenOffice (which exports only to *.doc format) or LibreOffice (which exports to either format).

Cleaning the html

Now go to the website Word2CleanHtml.com and paste your book (*.doc or *.docx) into the provided window. (There are a dozen similar sites, if Word2Clean is offline at the moment, and at least one plug-in that does the same job.) You can do this as a single file or as individual chapters. I favor a single file, but my books are mostly modest in size, with the longest being about 140,000 words. As I recall, I had to make three passes through Word2CleanHtml with that book, then stitch the three html files together.

Beneath the window are six options, the first two and the last of which are already checked. I also check the third option, "Replace non-ascii with Html equivalents."

Now click on the button to **convert to clean html**. In an instant, your book is stripped of all the excess instructions that your word processor inserted unseen into your book. Special formatting, like italics or boldface, is retained, and all paragraphs should begin with a **<p>** tag and be closed off by a **</p>**.

Paste this "clean html" into **Notepad++** or other text editor, or straight into Sigil Code View if you have advanced that far. If you are using Notepad++, you will instantly see the beauty of this software, which displays those paragraph tags in blue, so you can quickly check to see that every time one is opened, it is also closed. (Sigil now also provides this service, though the color cues are less dramatic.)

Tweaking the clean html

The result is not perfect, alas. I used the search function in Notepad++ to find the double asterisks in front of the chapter titles, and I replaced it with something like this, depending on the chapter:

<h2 id="chapter06">

I no longer have to do this, since Sigil handles the table of contents very nicely on its own. The opening and closing **h2** tags are all you really need. They ensure that the heading will appear in the desired size, in italics, centered on the page, and with an anchor for the hot-linked chapter title in the table of contents. In Sigil, you can do this by marking the title with your mouse, then clicking on the **h2** icon in the toolbar menu.

Next I changed the first paragraph of this chapter so that it began —

<p class="first"><span
class="smallcap">PROBABLY YOU

WROTE</span>

— which utilizes two other paragraph classes. One calls up the no-indent style traditionally used in the opening paragraph of a chapter or major section, and the other calls up the boldfaced span. I have used a few other paragraph classes in this chapter, including the **blockcenter** style that produced the monospaced examples above. Very likely, however, those are flourishes that you are willing to put forward to another day.

Once in a while, Word2CleanHtml will insert a paragraph tag where none is wanted, especially if a punctuation mark follows a boldfaced or italicized word. Notepad++ makes it easy to spot these unnecessary paragraphs and to fix them by deleting the extra tags. Similarly, the software once gave me paragraph tags reading **<p class="normal">**, obliging me to do a find-and-replace to strip them down to a plain **<p>**. (That happened to be a doc file from OpenOffice Writer.)

In addition to editing the chapter titles and first-paragraph classes, you may want to use sub-heads in your book. These are covered in the next chapter. For now, just save your cleaned-up html as a separate file in your book folder.

Or if you just can't wait, go ahead and open the book framework created in Step 1. Copy the entire book file to your computer's Clipboard utility, then paste it into the framework at the spot indicated. You can then admire it in your web browser. (In Notepad++, click on **Run** and choose your favorite browser.) The browser is an excellent place to proof your work. Be aware, however, that it displays the book differently than will an e-book device. When I opened the html of this chapter in Google Chrome, it ignored most of the styling, and it displayed the quotes and em dashes incorrectly, because it didn't have access to my style sheet. Still, it's a useful step for checking the content of your book.

Other converters for Word

I've used Word2Clean for all my books since I converted to the epub format. As mentioned earlier, however, there are other online sites offering similar services. And if you have a recent version of Word (2007 onward), you can download a free add-in from the Dutch software developer who goes by the web name of Toxaris. Among other tricks, it will convert Word to html. The add-in gets very good reviews, though I can't get it to work on my desktop computer. You can download the most recent version from **Toxaris.nl** (in English, I'm happy to say). It's for Windows only, however.

Step 6 - Heads and Sub-Heads

SINCE WE ARE on the subject of headings, I will use all three levels in this chapter. The chapter title above is level **<h2>**, and the html reads like this:

<h2 id="chapter07"> Step 6 - Heads and Sub-Heads</h2>

As defined in the style sheet, an h2 head is set at 150 percent of the text size, is italicized, and is dropped one line from the top of the screen. I think this makes a handsome chapter title.

The identifier **id="chapter07"** is the anchor for the hotlink in the table of contents, so that if you click on the chapter title, you will be taken right to this spot. (The anchor is required only if you upload your book as a single file. You will probably stop including anchors after a while, since you can let Sigil make this connection for you, as you split the book into multiple files.)

Here Is an H3 Heading

If your subject is technical or otherwise complicated, you can break the chapters into sections, as I have done in this book. Below is the html for a major section break, as shown above:

<h3>Here Is an H3 Heading</h3>

Here, the type size is 125 percent of the text, is dropped one line from the text above, and is centered on the page. I use an "up" style for these headings, capitalizing words just as I would for the chapter title. You might prefer the more informal "down" style, with only the first letter and proper nouns capitalized.

And here is an h4 sub-head

For a less important section, you can use a similar heading that is set flush against the left margin. I like this sort of "breakhead," as we called it in the newspaper business. Its purpose is mostly to break the gray flow of type on a page. Here's the html:

<h4>And here is an h4 sub-head</h4>

Here too, the typeface size is 125 percent of normal text, which works out well in digital books. (I opt for a slightly smaller font for this print edition.) The sub-head is flush to the left margin, and I use a "down" style, capitalizing the words just as I would in the text.

You should now go through your book file, in Notepad++ or whatever other text editor you are using, and add the opening and closing tags for the chapter titles and lesser headings that you want to use. In the case of the chapter titles, you might want to check that they contain the anchor that enables the table of contents to find them.

And note that if there are headings you *don't* want to appear in the Table of Contents, you can simply use the paragraph class of "medium" instead of an <h2> head, or "small" instead of <h3>. They will look exactly the same in the finished book, but they won't be part of the TOC hierarchy. I usually do this in the case of the **About the Author** section, as described in Step 7.

Again, let me emphasize that once you are working in Sigil, much of this work will be automated for you. The software can generate your table of contents, so you needn't build the hotlinks or lay down the anchors. And if you have a line of text that you want to mark as a heading, all you'll have to do is highlight it with your mouse, then click on the appropriate icon in the top menu. Sigil provides six heading levels, from h1 to h6, though my style sheet uses only h2, h3, and h4. If you should ever need a lesser breakhead than h4, you can simply start a paragraph with a boldface phrase, followed by a full stop.

Step 7 - The Copyright and Author Pages

YOU WILL NO DOUBT build this section while you're finishing your book in Microsoft Word or other word processor. I treat it as a separate step because there are some points I want to make that aren't always obvious to the beginning e-book publisher.

The most important point: you can and probably should put the copyright information at the *back* of your e-book and not where it usually appears in a print edition, immediately following the title page. The same is true of most of the introductory material that clutters up the first dozen or so pages of many books. My e-books start out like this: a title page, a table of contents, perhaps a frontispiece (this book has one), and then the first page of the first chapter. That's a bow to the valuable preview or sample or "Look Inside" provided by some online bookstores and lending libraries. It's your very best opportunity to make a sale. The sample typically consists of the first 10 percent of the *text* of your book, and you don't want to waste that 10 percent on clearing your throat before the good stuff begins.

An increasing number of mainstream publishers are following suit, moving the inessential stuff to the back of the book. And in the case of digital editions, that often includes the copyright information. There is no requirement that it should be at the front, though we've always done it that way. As a matter of fact, since e-books generally open at the first page of text, the reader is likely never to see that preliminary stuff anyhow, and is actually more likely to read it if it's at the back!

In 2017, Amazon introduced a new version of Look Inside, one that more closely resembles the purchased book. Among other things, the sample of most books now begins with the first text page of the first chapter, skipping everything that comes before. This seems to affect more than half of the e-books on the US store; the others follow the old Look Inside rules. In the meantime, I see no reason to change my preferred layout.

You will find my copyright information on page 4 of this print edition. Below is the html that I used in the e-book, and which you are welcome to adapt to your own use. It begins with a standard chapter head:

\<h2 id="copy">Copyright\</h2>

Which is followed by a brief declaration of my rights to the book:

\<p class="first">\<span class="smallcap">NOTJOHN’S GUIDE\</span> to E-Book Formatting copyright © 2013, 2020 by Enjay Press. Eleventh edition January 2020. Illustrations by the author and from the public domain. All rights reserved. No part of this book may be reproduced in any format, print or electronic, without permission in writing from the copyright holders. For further information, email \<b>notjohnkdp\</b> at \<b>gmail.com\</b>.\</p>

You can add to that, of course, and most publishers do. But I like to keep it simple. And before you ask: yes, in most cases it is sufficient to *assert* your copyright. You may want to register your book with the Library of Congress or the equivalent agency in your own country, but for most author-publishers this isn't a good investment. You own the copyright by virtue of having written the book, and that's an end to it. (Yes, with a registered copyright you have additional protection, but really — could you afford the bother and expense of filing a suit?) Note that Amazon puts the date of first publication on the book's store page, and it is very good at fending off pirates.

I should add that the strange-looking **©** is the html tag for the international copyright symbol, which looks like this: ©.

About the Author

I like to finish off my books with a short autobiography, emphasizing the bits that relate to the subject at hand, and ending with a list of digital editions and perhaps a teaser excerpt from one of them. Here is how you might introduce such a section, which follows right after the copyright notice:

<p class="medium">About the Author</p>

What I have done here is switch to the paragraph class devised for the title page, so it won't be picked up as a separate entry in the table of contents. Yet it will look just the same on the e-book screen as an h2 heading. This is just a minor refinement, and if you don't want to bother with it, that's fine. I only bring it up because it seems to me that having too many distinct chapters at the end of the book might puzzle the reader. You'll notice that in the Table of Contents for the e-book, I similarly combined the two concluding sections into a single entry, but substituting "Was This Book Helpful?" for "About the Author." Here's the html:

```
<p class="center">
<href="../Text/Section0014.xhtml#copy">
Copyright - Was This Book Helpful? </a></p>
```

Works for me!

Note that in the digital edition of this Guide, I haven't used an Author section, since "Notjohn" is an alias and, what's more, he doesn't have any other books on offer.

Step 8 - Adding Illustrations

IF YOU HAVE NO illustrations in your book, you've simplified your task a great deal, and you can skip this chapter. Otherwise, you need to become familiar with at least one of those style sheet "divisions," the one called **div.image**, and perhaps the one for a caption. But first let me discourage you from employing captions in your e-book. Though I captioned some of the illustrations in this Guide, I avoid them in most of my books. Instead I try to explain them (and perhaps link to them) in the text — if at all possible, *before* the image appears.

Furthermore, as I did in this book, I like to insert images *between* chapters, rather than sprinkle them through the text. There are reasons for doing this. In an e-book, unlike a print edition, you can't know where an image is going to fall. If you insert it into the text, very likely it will be preceded by an incomplete page, perhaps half a page, perhaps just a few lines. Far better to let the chapter complete itself, then devote the following page to the illustration. (You might also consider clustering all the illustrations in the middle of the book.)

Much the same is true of the caption. Even though you might "square off" the image sufficiently to allow room for a caption on the traditional Kindle — or Nook or iPad or Kobo Reader — held vertically, you can't be certain that the reader will choose to view it that way. He or she may have set the gadget to landscape (horizontal) mode. So avoid captions if you can. Often you can merge the information into the preceding text. I don't always follow this advice myself, but setting the illustration off in a file of its own at least ensures that some or all of the caption is on a page of its own, and not mixed with the text.

The Image

There are two principal types of image that you are likely to employ in your e-books. The most common has the **jpg** extension, pronounced "jay-peg" and best suited for photographs. The other is a **gif**, pronounced "jiff," used for drawings and other line art. In this Guide, the photo of the Sony Data Discman on page 6 is a jpg, while the screenshot on page 57 is a gif. Here is the html for the Discman page:

<div class="image" id="disc"> <img alt="Sony Data Discman" src="../Images/discman.jpg" width="100%"> </div>

Okay, let's break that down. First there is **div class ="image"** which calls up the appropriate layout from the style sheet. The image will be centered horizontally on the page, with a small space between the bottom of the image and the line that follows it, in case it is followed by a caption or a paragraph of text.

Next you see **id="disc"**, the identifier or **anchor** that enables a hyperlink to find the right place in the book. This is necessary only if you build your e-book as a single file and you plan to point to the illustration in the table of contents or somewhere in the text. Here again, Sigil can save you much work. If you put each image in a separate file, as the software encourages you to do, Sigil can find it without an anchor.

The next bit of information is **alt="Sony Data Discman"**, a courtesy to sight-impaired readers. Many e-reader devices have an audio option, enabling the user to let the gadget speak the text aloud. Though the voice sounds a bit stilted, the result is really very good, and indeed I sometimes use it when proofreading a book. Without the **alt=** instruction, the read-aloud feature wouldn't know what to do with a photograph. Here, it will speak the alternative phrase. You don't *have* to include it, but there are readers who will thank you for it.

Then comes **img src="../Images/discman.jpg"**, which tells the software to look for the jpg named "discman" in Sigil's Images folder (because the target is preceded by *../Images/)*. If you are brave enough to write the html entirely by yourself, and you plan to upload the book as a single file, then all you need is the name of the image: *img src="discman.jpg"*. (Be careful with the spelling! *Src* is an abbreviation for *source*, but people have a tendency to spell it *scr*. And it's hard to spot the mistake when you're proof-reading. I know; I have done this myself, more than once.)

Finally, there is the instruction **width="100%"**. I began doing this with the introduction of high-resolution devices like Amazon's Fire tablets, the Kindle Paperwhite and Voyage, and Apple's iPad and other tablets. Amazon used to recommend that full-page images be 450 pixels wide. That was upped to 600 pixels when the second generation of e-readers came along. Today, the help pages merely say that images should be "high resolution" — but what does that mean, exactly?

Of dots and pixels

Images on an electronic screen are measured in **pixels**, while those on the printed page are measured in **dots**. (If you look closely at a newspaper, you can actually see the dots in a photograph.) Those are useful terms for people who work with images, but the difference between a dot and a pixel has no significance for an e-book publisher: just think of them as interchangeable.

I use **Photoshop Elements** to manipulate images, while others prefer **Paint Shop Pro**. They aren't cheap (about $70 if you look around), but are worth the investment if you plan to do a lot of formatting. Otherwise I suggest you download the free and excellent **IrfanView**, which was recommended to me when I bought a Canon scanner whose included software proved to be just about useless. It worked beautifully for that purpose, and now I actually prefer it for many tasks formerly assigned to Photoshop, because it loads so quickly. Download it from IrfanView.com and use it to open any jpeg or other image in your computer. (If you don't have one, just grab one off the internet.) Using the top menu, click on *File > Open*, then explore your options. For example, click on *Image > Resize/Resample*, which brings up a trove of information including its dimensions. I'm looking at a jpeg 1600 pixels wide by 1200 pixels tall, which I can reduce to a more reasonable size by typing 800 into the Width box.

But does that qualify as "high resolution"? Well, no, and Amazon in its Publishing Guidelines actually suggests that every full-width image be sized at 3200 pixels, which in my opinion is absurd. Yes, if you enlarge the images in this Guide enough, they will blur, but so what? They're good enough for government work, as we used to say in the defense industry. The same is true of photos that I published in 2008, when Amazon was telling us to keep our images down to 450 pixels wide. Indeed, I still compress jpegs and gifs to the 127 kilobytes that Amazon used to recommend, using the "save for web" option in Photoshop. (IrfanView has a similar option, though it requires a plug-in you can download from the software's website.) The cost saving is huge. Amazon charges a download fee of 15 cents per megabyte if you choose its

70 percent royalty. I can put ten 127 KB images in a book and keep the download fee at under 30 cents. For a grayscale image, you can figure one byte per pixel, so if you aren't careful you can wind up with a download fee that exceeds the price of your book, meaning that your only option is to settle for the 35 percent royalty. (No other online bookseller levies a download fee.)

Amazon also suggests that you save your images at a resolution of 300 ppi (pixels per inch). There is much confusion on the e-book publishing forums about this. In fact, it doesn't makes the slightest difference: *The only thing that matters is the image's actual height and width in pixels.*

Small images

And sometimes you might actually *want* a small image! My title page includes a colophon or icon for Notjohn Press. Below is the html that called it up, containing the instruction **width="15%"**. Just as you can push images to fill a large screen, you can shrink them to limit their screen space.

```
<div class="icon"><img
src="../Images/openbook.gif" width="15%"
alt="Enjay Press"></a></div>
```

I used the icon class in another book, where I wanted a sunburst to separate one section of the text from another. And you could adapt this html instruction to display a small portrait of the author or thumbnails of your other books. Find a size that pleases you, but you probably won't want to go larger than width="50%" because it limits the space available for text, and also because widths between 50% and 100% has been known to fail on some devices.

Here for example is a style that I used successfully on another of my books, when I needed thumbnail images (which editors call "mug shots") of several individuals with the text flowing around them:

```
div.mug {
width:20%;
height:auto;
float:left;
margin-right:0.5em;
}
```

This too is a division, so is called up by **<div class ="mug">**, immediately following the paragraph style **<p class="first">**. The mug shot or thumbnail is positioned against the left margin, with the text filling the rest of the screen.

Be aware that smaller images will fail on some of the oldest e-readers. I don't regard this as a disabling problem — "not a ditch to die in," as the saying goes. You can minimize the risk by sizing the image appropriately. My colophon, for example, is 100 pixels wide. It's oversized on the old devices, but not unacceptably so. (At one time, it was also oversized on the Look Inside sample, but this is no longer the case.)

The Caption

Okay, you're planning to ignore my advice and add a caption to your illustration. No problem! For the frontispiece, I could have followed the image division with this:

<div class="caption">The Sony Data Discman, circa 1992</div>

Which would have appeared on the Kindle page like this:

The Sony Data Discman, circa 1992

Thus, obeying the instructions in the style sheet, our caption is presented in italics; it is centered horizontally on the page; and it is followed by a blank line, just in case there might be text following on the same page. (Always be aware that the caption and the blank line might force all or part of it onto the next e-book "page.")

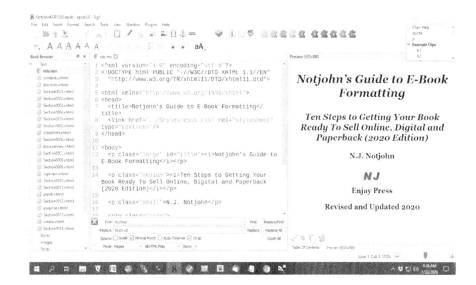

Sigil opened to this book's title page. Across the top are several menu lines, plus (on the right) a menu of clips that I often use. Below those are three panels. The narrow Book Browser lists each each chapter or other section as a separate file. Then comes my html file in Code View, where I do all my work. On the right is Preview, showing the book as it will appear in the e-reader or app. Any change made in Code View immediately shows up in the Preview panel. WYSIWYG!

Step 9 - Sigil Works Its Magic

OKAY! YOU HAVE all the pieces in place, and it only remains to put them together. If you have been tipping the pieces into the framework as you went along — preferably in NoteTab, Notepad++, or a close equivalent — then you are ready for the next step. If not, you ought to do it now. Remember to save it as an ***.htm** file instead of with a *.txt extension.

And before you go any further, why not see your book as the web page it really is? Open up your web browser — I mostly use Google Chrome — and press Control-O for "open." Now browse to the folder where your book lives and click or double-click on the html file containing it. Beautiful, isn't it? (The formatting will be web standard — an extra space between paragraphs, for example — because your style sheet is still missing.) This is also a grand opportunity to look for any errors like an unclosed boldface tag.

And you might want to **validate** your html file. You can get a thorough check at Validator.W3.Org online. Choose the option to **Validate by File Upload**, browse to your book file, and upload it. This can be a terrifying moment. Likely the software will find dozens of errors and warnings: I had thirty-three when I first validated this Guide. Most will be of no importance. For example, four or five of my errors were the use of **B&N** with a bare ampersand as typed on the keyboard, while the validator wanted to see the "html entity" — **&** — which I let Sigil fix. Other flags had to do with the lack of coding instructions at the top of my document, which lack Sigil also remedied.

Neither of these errors would have affected the document in the way it displayed as a web page or as it converted to an e-book. However, some errors had to do with an unclosed html tag, or a closing tag that was repeated. If I had looked at the file more closely in Notepad++, with its color display, I would have found most of them. As it was, I searched for them in the html file, guided by the validator, and fixed them there.

Introducing Sigil

In the folder or directory devoted to your book, you now have a file with the extension ***.htm** (or *.html), a style sheet with the extension ***.css**, and perhaps one or more images with the extension ***.jpg** or ***.gif**.

Next, go to "Github.Com/Sigil-Ebook/Sigil/releases" and download the latest version of Sigil. (Or search for "latest Sigil version" and follow the Github link.) At this writing, it's 1.0.0, a brand-new release. I have always found it a mistake to buy an automobile in its first model year, and I apply the same logic to software. So I built the digital edition of this book with Sigil 0.9.18, a safe and solid version that was last updated in September 2019. It is still available on the Github site. You probably want the Setup.exe file for Windows. If you use a Mac or Linux operating system, skip down to the bottom the page for the instructions.

When I downloaded Sigil , my browser raised a great fuss, warning me of the dangers posed by unrecognized software, and when I installed it, my computer likewise fretted that I was endangering its health. If this happens to you, I'm sorry, but it really is safe to proceed. Sigil installs like any other software.

On the same Github page, there's a lot about "bug fixes" and "new features," which you can skip. But by all means download the **FlightCrew plug-in**, also at the bottom of the page. This handy validator used to be an integral part of Sigil, but is now separate from it. With Sigil already on my computer, I found that FlightCrew installed itself without intervention from me. To reach it while working in Sigil, go to **Plugins > Validation > FlightCrew** on Sigil's top menu bar. While there, you can use **Manage Plugin** to assign the validator to one of the several icons to the right of the middle menu bar, numbered 1 to 10 in Sigil 0.9.18. Sigil's developers now urge us to download Epubcheck as a more reliable validator, but haven't yet provided a link to it on this page.

Sigil in action

Sigil is in a constant state of revision, as the volunteer developers improve its ability to handle the emerging standard of **epub3**. Personally, I see no reason to abandon the epub2 format that I have been using since 2012. So the next thing I did, after installing FlightCrew, was to go to **Edit > Preferences > General Settings** on the top menu bar and make sure that Version 2 was selected.

When you open Sigil for the first time, you will see a blank html file that looks like this:

```
<?xml version="1.0" encoding="utf-8"?>
<!DOCTYPE html PUBLIC "-//W3C//DTD
XHTML 1.1//EN"
"http://www.w3.org/TR/xhtml11/DTD/xhtml11
.dtd">

<html
xmlns="http://www.w3.org/1999/xhtml">
<head>
<title></title>
```

```
</head>
<body>
<p> </p>
</body>
</html>
```

That is the skeleton of your book. There are two ways to put flesh on its bones. If you did a first-class job with building your book's html file, you can simply erase Sigil's framework and replace it with your book. Or you can take my shortcut, which is to highlight the line that reads *<p> </p>* and replace it with the cleaned-up html that you acquired in Step 5. Just paste it in.

A warning: *Sigil doesn't save your work on its own*, so you could lose hours of work if your computer suddenly shuts down. Make it a habit to use **Control** + **S** at regular intervals (or **File** > **Save** on the top menu). You should also set up a Dropbox account, or use another backup system, to save a copy of your book file off-site. Sigil has an especially convenient **File > Save a Copy** option for just this purpose. I do this at least once a day, and often several times. I also change the file name every couple of days, which enables me to retrace my steps if I ever lose my way.

What you see is what you get

I set up the program as three panels side by side, with a narrow **Book Browser** on the left. This is the list of all the files in my book, which by now number twenty-four. The large central panel is the **Code View** displaying my html. And, on the right, is the **Preview** that has turned Sigil into a WYSIWYG editor: what you see is what you get. See the screenshot that opens this chapter.

I do most of my editing in Code View, though when I was getting accustomed to the software I first revised the html in my text editor, then pasted it into Sigil. But you can certainly make minor changes in Code View, and in time you will be comfortable enough to do much of your work there. Any change you make will promptly be displayed in the Preview. If you mess up, Preview waves a red warning flag, and the text ends where the bad html was entered — or not entered, since the most common editing error is the lack of a closing tag.

You may have to fuss a bit before the three panels line up properly. Sometimes the outside panels want to overlay the central one, and you must shuffle them about. Obviously it helps if you have a wide monitor. By going to **Edit > Preferences > Appearance**, you can set the typeface and size that works best for you; I am using 16 point Georgia in Preview and 12 point Liberation Mono in Code View.

Styling your book

In the large central panel, your entire book will be laid out from beginning to end, with the html tags visible. Meanwhile, in the Preview panel on the right, your book is displayed as it would be on a Kindle or other e-reader. The first task is to add your style sheet and link it to the html. (If you used the Plan B basic framework, a simplified style sheet is already in place, and you can skip this step.) In the narrow Book Browser panel on the left, right-click on the **Styles** folder and choose **Add Existing Files**. This opens a window in which you can navigate to your book folder and select your style sheet, which I am assuming is named *epub.css*.

Your html book file, as opened in Sigil Code View, will have some ready-made lines at the top, including a heading that looks like this:

<head>

```
<title></title>
</head>
```

This is where you link the style sheet to your html. You should also add your book title if it isn't already there. You will end up with something like this:

```
<head>
<title>Book Title Here</title>
<link href="../Styles/epub.css"
rel="stylesheet" type="text/css"/>
</head>
```

If you used my full e-book framework, this language is already in place. Otherwise, add it now. Since editing in Code View is likely to be hazardous at first, you might want to do this tinkering in a text editor, then copy and paste it. Or copy and paste it straight from my blog, then overwrite *Book Title Here* with the name of your book.

From one file to many

Working in Code View, place your mouse cursor on the first empty space following the last bit of html on the title page. In the case of this book, it's just after the **</p>** following the year of publication. Left-click on the space immediately to the right of that closing tag. Now move the mouse cursor to the second menu row, the one with icons. About in the middle of the row is an icon showing one large and two small pages: one page into two! If you let the cursor hover over that icon, a window should appear, saying *Split At Cursor*. Click on it! (Or, on the top menu line, click on **Edit > Split At Cursor**.)

When I did this, I wound up with two files, the first containing just the title page, the second containing the rest of the book and labeled *Section 0001.xhtml*. It doesn't make the slightest difference what the files are named — I later named the first one title.htm and the second contents.xhtml.

And so I continued through the book, creating a new file at the end of the most recent one, and also creating a new file for each image, so that it too will stand by itself. (Splitting off images is not strictly necessary, but I like the result.) The only sections that I didn't split were the final two, which I treated as a single chapter.

Save your epub file before moving on to the next step. I am paranoid about saving and backing up my book files. Just in case the house should burn down while I'm away from home, I also have a Dropbox account that has no other purpose than to hold versions of my books as I work on them. This has the additional advantage that I can work on a project anywhere in the world, by logging on to Dropbox and downloading the latest draft. Indeed, that's how much of this book has been revised in the past, on the annual ski week in Colorado.

The metadata

Metadata is another of those terms that don't make a whole lot of sense. (If you really want to know, "metadata" is a set of data that gives information *about other data*. Really!) All you need do is plug in a few essential details. On Sigil's topmost menu, click on **Tools > Metadata Editor**. A window opens with lines for the book title, author name, and language, with the last already set to English. That's really all you need, but I usually click on **Add Basic** to add the **Publisher**, which in this case is Enjay Press. (You can type the information into the column marked **Value**.) Next I click on **Add Role**. I run down the list to **Copyright Holder** and — again in the value column — I type in the relevant information, which in my case is "2020 by Enjay Press."

When you close the metadata tool, Sigil adds the information to a file called **content.opf**, with the extension standing for **Open Packaging Format**. The OPF file is a required part of every epub, and since 2011 has been a required part of every Kindle e-book as well.

Building the logical TOC

By "logical," the geeks mean a virtual table of contents that does not appear in the text of the book, but can be accessed by the e-book software if you want to move to a different chapter or section. The information (stored in a file called **toc.ncx**, with the extension standing for **Navigation Control for Xhtml**) is likewise mandatory. I regularly use the logical TOC on my Kindle Fire tablet, and I suspect that others do as well, since it's easier to reach than going back to the actual or html table of contents at the front of the book.

Right! Go to **Tools** > **Table of Contents** > **Generate Table of Contents**, and Sigil opens up a window with the headings shown, a box to the right of each, and a checkmark in the box. You can remove the checkmark from any heading you don't want to include.

If you ignore my advice and use headings for your title page, you will of course remove them from the logical TOC. At the present time, that will cause no harm, but I don't trust that this will always be the case. Some day, perhaps, headings instead of paragraph styles on the title page might cause the book to fail validation.

In the case of this Guide, I will leave all the checkmarks in place, including my actual TOC — the one shown at the front of this book. I figure that the logical TOC should be as detailed as possible, since this is a fairly technical publication, and people will be referring back to it, and reading sections out of order.

You can edit the name of any chapter or division, and by using the left or right arrow you can make it more important or less important. If you have carefully constructed your book file, I don't see any point in messing with it here. Click "OK" and move on. (Note that if you later change the wording of any chapter title or lesser heading, you should go back to the "Generate" tool again. Usually it's enough just to click the "OK" button, which saves the new wording in the toc.ncx file. If you don't do this, you will get an error the next time you use Flight Crew or other validator.)

Laying down the markers

On the left of your monitor, the **Book Browser** shows all the files you have created in building your epub. (If you don't see it, go to **View > Book Browser** and it will appear.) If you right-click on any file in this list, a menu opens up that allows you, among other options, to **Add Semantics**. (Another awful term. I would have said "markers.") And if you left-click on this option, a second list opens up, showing the many categories that you can assign to any given page in your book.

I like to keep things simple, so I only mark four categories: **Cover**, **Title Page**, **Table of Contents**, and **Copyright Page**. "Text" is another option, but one that I ignore. In an epub, the book is supposed to begin at the file marked with this semantic. And perhaps it does, in a Kobo or similar reader. But the default opening of a Kindle book seems to be the first page of text following the table of contents. And Amazon itself sets that starting point (which it calls the **SRL** or Start Reading Location) during the publishing process, *after* you have finished with the book. If you want, you can of course add the Text semantic to the file where Amazon expects to see it.

But for reasons of my own, I omit the SRL. That's to take advange of the Look Inside feature on the Amazon store. I am a strong believer that the experience of reading a book begins with its cover, so I always page back to see the cover, then step forward through the title page, table of contents, and whatever else the publisher chooses to show me. And I have found that, if I omit the SRL, the Look Inside sample will often (not always, alas, and perhaps not even half the time) open at the cover. The purchased book unfortunately will not, which is why so many Kindle users can't tell you the author of the book they're reading, or even its title.

Add the cover

Amazon doesn't require an "included cover" for Kindle books. Instead, the image that you upload as the **Kindle eBook Cover** (second step on the second tab of the publishing process) will be reduced in size and inserted at the front of the book. However, you should sell your book on other platforms as well, especially for the Apple, Kobo, and Barnes & Noble bookstores, and for those you should include a cover. There is no standard for this image. I favor something a bit more generous than my other inside images, say 1000 x 1500 pixels. The result looks good to me, whether viewed on a B&N Nook or an Apple iPad. To add the cover in Sigil, right-click on the folder titled **Images**, then go to **Add Existing Files**. A window pops up, allowing you to search for the modified cover image. Once it has been added to the folder, click on **Tools** in the top menu, and choose the first option, **Add Cover**. That opens a view of the *Images* folder, where you can select the image you just added. Use the Semantics tool to mark it as **Cover**, though you may find that it is already so labeled.

On rare occasions, I have wound up with *two* covers in the Kindle edition. To avoid that, I delete the included cover in the KDP version, henceforth maintaining one version of the book for Amazon (notjohnkdp.epub) and another for the rest of the world (notjohnd2d.epub, because most of those are sold through the Draft2Digital "aggregator.")

Finishing Up

Remember that there is no auto-save in Sigil. At regular intervals — whenever you have done work that you don't want to lose, even if that means every paragraph — go **Ctrl-S** to save it to disk. And at the end of every working session, or more frequently, save a backup copy to an external hard drive or to a service like Dropbox.

And Prettify it!

No offense intended, but your html is probably a bit of a mess. Among Sigil's built-in tools is one that cleans up messes. On the top menu row, click on **Tools > Reformat Html > Mend and Prettify All HTML Files**. That's all there is to it. In older versions of Sigil, you could set this feature to operate every time you saved a book file, but now it must be done manually. Do it every day, at the very least, before you save your backup copy.

Mending and prettifying the code should change nothing. But it will fix minor errors, such as an omitted end-paragraph tag, and it will make the html markup look better, closing up gaps and improving the spacing of paragraphs, so that the text is easier to read and errors easier to spot. I have automated this process by assigning a keyboard command to it. On the top menu, go to **Edit > Preferences > Keyboard Shortcuts**. One of the options is the above mentioned **Mend and Prettify**. Click on it to highlight the line, then type your favored shortcut (I use *Alt+P*) in the window at the bottom. Press the keys; don't write the actual letters. (In my case, I tapped the *Alt* key, then the *p*.) Click on **Assign**, and you're done.

And validate, validate, validate!

I trust you have already added the FlightCrew validator, as described earlier. You can activate it by clicking on **Plugins** > **Validation** > **FlightCrew** on the top menu, or by clicking on the appropriate icon on the right side of the second menu row if you used that option. Again, run the validator every day at the very least, after you finish your work and before you save the backup copy. After FlightCrew runs, a new panel opens at the bottom of your monitor with the validation results. Hopefully you will have no errors. If you do, you'll have to fix them — see below.

Even after FlightCrew gives my book a clean bill of health, I go one step further and upload the entire file to **Epubcheck** at Validator.IDPF.Org online. I find that cleaning up a book by running it though Word2Clean-Html, as recommended in Step 5, occasionally leaves an errant and empty tag in the book, trying to call up an image or a page that doesn't exist. If there is such an error, Epubcheck specifies what file it's in and the line number, so it's an easy matter to find the offending tag and remove it. I've had this happen several times, so it seems that FlightCrew misses the error. It's important that your book pass Epubcheck, because otherwise it will be refused by Apple.

As an alternative to the online service, look for and download a free utility called Pagina Epub Checker, by the German software developer Tobias Fischer. I ran it just now and found that this book has no problems whatever.

Looking for help

If you haven't already downloaded the *Sigil User's Guide*, you should do it now. If you click on **Help > User Guide** in the top menu line, you will be taken to a page called "Documentation" that doesn't actually contain the User Guide, but does have a link to it at the Github repository. It comes as an epub, which you can view in Sigil itself or in the Adobe Digital Editions software. (ADE is a useful addition to your toolkit, since it is a recognized standard for previewing epubs.) I used it just this morning to learn how to set a new keyboard shortcut.

The KDP Community has a sub-forum dedicated to formatting, which I visit almost every day if I'm not on the road. The help level here can vary hugely, and few of the regulars link to their books, so it's hard to judge how seriously to take their advice. If all else fails, the Sigil forum at MobileRead.Com should be your next port of call. Be aware that the geek level among the regular posters is rather high, and they can be rough on those who don't speak their language, or who have the temerity to be critical of the software. If that puts you off, you can always post a question on my blog, and I will do my best to answer it. I'm not as smart as they are, but I strive to be kinder.

All right! Congratulations — your book is ready to publish.

Step 10 - Getting Your Book Online

W ITH A VALID EPUB, you should have no trouble uploading to Kindle Direct Publishing, to an aggregator like Draft2Digital, or to Amazon's competitors individually. (Well, Apple and Google Play can be a challenge.) I strongly advise you not to give Amazon exclusive rights to your book. Almost certainly you will find more readers, and you'll probably earn more money, by having it available on Kobo, Apple, and Barnes & Noble, to name just the most promising retail alternatives. I also like having my books on Scribd, a subscription service that pays better than Amazon's Kindle Unlimited; and on Overdrive, which serves public libraries in the United States and elsewhere. (One of my e-books is available in 27 Massachusetts libraries, which is quite a thrill, since I double my price for library sales.)

A 2017 survey suggested that Amazon sold about 80 percent of the e-books purchased in the English-speaking world, with Apple accounting for 10 percent, Barnes & Noble 3 percent, and Kobo 2 percent. Google Play and other minor players got smaller shares. Well, maybe. Amazon grossly inflates its market share by counting "sales" of its own imprints. Most of these are freebies download by its *95 million Prime subscribers*, yet each is counted as a purchase. Similarly, whenever a subscriber to its Kindle Unlimited library borrows a book, that is also a sale, even if the subscriber reads just a few pages — or none! Together, these little deceptions make Amazon's best-seller lists so unreliable as to be fraudulent.

My own experience has been more varied. Yes, my split between Amazon and the rest is about 80/20. But Kobo is my second-best market, after Amazon, probably because last year it became the distributor of e-books to Walmart's online store. Apple is in third place, and Barnes & Noble is fourth. (The differences are slight.)

So let's assume that Amazon sells 80 percent of our e-books. That means we're leaving a lot of books on the table if we commit to KDP Select. True, you won't be eligible to enroll your book in the Kindle Unlimited lending library, but the returns there are paltry, less than half a cent for each page read. Even a full read for a 70,000-word book earns about half what the same book would bring if sold at a modest $2.99. (That happens to be my bottom price, which I reserve for very short books, 20,000 words or so, most of them expanded magazine articles or research papers.)

You may earn more by committing to Kindle Select if you write lengthy, easily-digested genre fiction, the sort most likely to be downloaded by KU subscribers. (Of all genres, erotica and "romantica," its less graphic cousin, are the most popular by far.) But in my opinion it's a bad strategy for authors to encourage a monopoly. Always remember that Amazon is in business to enrich itself, not us. Take note of this: When the Kindle self-publishing platform was launched in 2007, Amazon paid us a 35 percent royalty. And note that this isn't really a *royalty*. Rather, it's a share of the *revenue*, out of which we must pay our publishing expenses and reimburse ourselves for the work we devote to formatting, publishing, and marketing.

In 2010 Apple changed everything by introducing its iBooks Store and the iBooks platform in competition to the KDP, with a "royalty" of 70 percent, which quickly became the standard, and one that Amazon was forced to match. In the lead-footed way of bureaucracies, the US government then sued *Apple* for price-fixing!

The day after the last competing e-tailer gives up the battle, I'm sure we will see 35 percent again. Or 25 percent, or worse. That is Amazon's business model: it turns up the heat very gradually, so that the frog doesn't understand it's being cooked until it's being served for dinner.... Besides, you probably know people who won't buy books from Amazon because it's the monster that ate their favorite Mom & Pop Bookstore. If you're not selling books that can be read on their favored e-reader — perhaps a Nook for the old folks, an iPad or smartphone for the young, or a Kobo Reader for hard-core techies and Walmart shoppers — those customers are lost to you forever.

Anyhow, can you really consider yourself an author if your work isn't for sale on the website of America's only remaining national chain of bookstores?

Kindle Direct Publishing

Nevertheless, Amazon is almost certainly going to be your most important e-book retailer, so this is where you should start. If you don't already have a KDP account, establish one now. You must use your real name even if you plan to publish under a pseudonym. Similarly, you must enter your home country tax identification number, mail address, and banking information. (Payoneer.com seems to be an adequate substitute if you live in a country where banking is too expensive or Amazon won't send electronic payments.) If you have questions, ask them at the **KDP Community** forums. You can use a made-up name here, by setting up a different Amazon account for the purpose, and many of us do just that.

Once your account is set up, go to your **Bookshelf**

and click on **Create a New Title > Kindle eBook** toward the top of the page. You are presented with three tabbed pages, the first of which is:

Kindle eBook Details

I think you should have your title, subtitle (a good subtitle is worth spending time on, for it is a powerful sales tool), and book description already keyed into a text editor such as Notepad. That way, you won't make mistakes when entering this vital information. It's very easy to get things wrong while typing online, and easy to overlook mistakes on a computer screen.

You first choose the **Language** of your book, with the default being English. Paste your **Book Title** into the next window and the **Subtitle** into the one following it. The title you enter here will appear on every Kindle page of your book, exactly as you entered it. (This stuff is called **metadata**, and is basically the same information you entered on Sigil's metadata tool .)

The next option allows you to enter a **Series** title and volume number, if this is one of several related books. In my experience, the volume number sometimes gets dropped, in which case you can email Support to have it added.

That is followed by a window in which you can enter an **Edition Number**. This happens to be the eleventh edition of this Guide, but the software demands a numeral, so I can't enter "eleventh" or even "11th." So I'll enter the year, 2020. The word *Edition* will be added by the software, and it will be followed on the Amazon page with the date of first publication.

Next is a window in which you enter the Author, who may be the individual on your driver's license or someone more fanciful. (Personal name on the left, family name on the right. You can use initials if you prefer, as I have done.) You can then add one or more **Contributors**, which usually means another Author, an Editor, or someone else who has added *significantly* to the book. If you want to acknowledge a formatter or cover designer, do it on the copyright page. And don't add your own name here, else it will be doubled on the Amazon store page. Another oddity of the KDP platform is that even if you're actually the book's Editor, that doesn't suffice: every book must have an Author.

That option is followed by the **Description** that will appear on the book's product page. Here again, it should be written in advance and pasted into the window. (If you use Notepad, turn off Word Wrap so that the entire description is one long line. Otherwise you'll have line breaks where you don't want them.) There is an art to writing this advertisement for yourself. You can tweak it later in your **Author Central** account as described in a later chapter, but be aware that if you ever republish the book, the KDP Description will overwrite the one from Author Central. (The KDP version also appears in any Amazon store where you don't maintain a separate Author Central account.)

Next you verify your **Publishing Rights**. I trust you are not messing about with public domain works, so check the first option: "I own the copyright and I hold the necessary publishing rights." If you wrote the book, you own the publishing rights unless you have actually sold them or given them to someone else.

Personally, I find the next few entries the most vexing part of the publishing process. You can and should add seven **Keywords**, either single words or short phrases. Think about what terms are likely to occur to someone searching for a book like yours. If the essential terms are already in your title or subtitle, you ought to put something less obvious here, because a search for those words will probably bring up your book anyhow. Thus I won't use the keyword "e-book" when I upload this version of my Guide — and by the same token, I most certainly *will* use the keyword "Kindle."

The same is true for **Categories**, which are the generally accepted fields of literature, from *Fiction, General* to *Non-Classifiable*, with the first and last categories being among the least desirable. If you write non-fiction, as I do, the chore is much more difficult. Only two categories are permitted, so you should think about them early on. Here, as in most research tasks, the internet is your friend. There are many blog posts about keywords and categories, and Amazon itself has a page about the chore.

I ignore the **Age and Grade Range**. I don't write children's books, and neither do I worry that any youngster would find my prose offensive.

Similarly, I make quick work of the **Publishing Option**. I don't see the point of setting a publishing date in the future — a "pre-order," as it's called. The best time to publish your book, it seems to me, is when it's ready. You won't believe how many self-publishers, pressured by the pre-order option, find they have released an unfinished book (or the wrong book!) into the wild. Pre-order is an option best reserved for writers with an established fan base or a hefty advertising campaign ready to go on publication day.

Okay! With the preliminaries out of the way, we can turn to KDP's second tab, which is:

Kindle eBook Content

Manuscript. Before you upload your book file, you must decide whether to choose **Digital Rights Man-**

agement, another wonderfully geeky term. DRM is an effort to prevent blatant piracy: your book is encrypted so that it can be read only on the device or devices registered to the buyer's account on Amazon. (It can however be loaned to someone for two weeks, for one time only, and for those two weeks it's not available to the person who owns it.) DRM is a contentious subject among e-book publishers, and also those e-book consumers who would prefer to have everything free for the taking. My own opinion is this: DRM won't stop a determined pirate, but it will stop casual distribution. It's like locking your house when you go on vacation: the determined thief will simply kick down the door, but the vast majority won't bother. *Why would you not opt for this protection*, slender though it may be?

Having selected DRM (or not), you are presented with a pitch for **Kindle Create**, which purports to do much of the work of formatting but actually is another dodge to lock you into the Amazon mini-verse, because it creates a "kpf" file that can be used nowhere else. You'll be doing yourself (and the rest of us) a favor if you ignore it. Instead, click on **Upload eBook manuscript**, find your epub file on your computer, and upload it. The system does a little shake and dance as the conversion begins. In most cases, the book "processes" in a very few minutes, and you will see a message something like this:

There's also an option at this point to see if the software has found typing mistakes in your book. I like this feature; it regularly catches stuff for me. (I had 47 errors when I first uploaded this file, but only two needed fixing. The others were differences of opinion, like spelling "smartphone" as one word or two. The reason there were no errors in this upload is that I had already flagged that and several other usages to be ignored.) If there are many errors, you can have Amazon email the list to you. Note that ignoring a suggestion will not cause your book to be rejected.

Kindle eBook Cover. Your cover is one of your most important sales tools, and I strongly advise you to have it done professionally. You can find a designer for $10-$15 on Fiverr (be prepared to turn down several), and you can probably find a talented professional for $150 or $200. Believe me: it is money well spent. An expensive cover doesn't guarantee that your book will be a best-seller, but virtually all best-sellers have expensive covers. The designer will provide you with a jpeg large enough and with sufficient detail (resolution) to make a good *Product Image* on the Amazon store. Despite the wisdom of your high-school English teacher, books have always been judged by their covers, and never more so than in our online age.

Generally I upload something on the order of 1000 pixels wide, 1500 pixels high. I like this 2/3 ratio better than the skinnier version that Amazon recommends. It looks more like a quality paperback cover, and it's an easy mental step-up from the print edition if you decide to go that route. (You probably should, for reasons I explain in my final chapter.) If you hire a cover designer, make this decision early, for it is easier and cheaper to create both covers at the same time. After the cover has been uploaded, it will appear as a small *thumbnail* image. Don't panic if it seems more or less illegible. The thumbnail is just that: a quick check to make sure you uploaded the correct image. It will look much better on the Amazon store page.

Your next step is the most critical in the publishing process:

Kindle eBook Preview. Until last summer, I was a strong believer in downloading and using Amazon's Kindle Previewer software. But I was still using the excellent 2.94 version, which had emulations for the older Kindles, for differing Kindles and Fire tablets, and even for Apple's iPhone and iPad (though these had to processed through the obnoxious iTunes software). Alas, my computer was wiped by a virus last summer, and Kindle Previewer 2.94 was among the programs that disappeared. I briefly looked at the current version, 3.36, but on my screen the emulations were too small to be read easily, and enlarging the typeface gave a false idea of what the page looked like on an actual Kindle, Fire tablet, or smartphone. And most of the emulations had disappeared! Finally, the small white letters on a black background struck me as depressingly ugly. If you don't mind it, by all means use it. If you are lucky enough to have the older Kindle Previewer on your computer, I envy you. But for the time being I will depend on the online preview option, which happily is the first one made available: just click on **Launch Previewer**.

Whatever you use, do spend a *lot* of time on this step, and don't let any outside pressure force you to hurry. This is especially true if you are serving as your own editor, formatter, and proofreader.

Kindle eBook ISBN. The last two items on this tab are grouped under the somewhat misleading topic of the International Standard Book Number. Almost every book printed in the past half-century has its own ISBN. You can acquire one for an e-book, too, but *you don't have to*. Most online bookstores provide their own inventory code for e-books, so the ISBN doesn't appear on the store page. More about ISBNs in the final chapter.

You really should have a unique and plausible publishing imprint, which you can enter in the window for **Publisher**. Even something as obvious as *Enjay Press* will serve to make a book seem reasonably professional, rather than the work of another anxious author desperate to have his or her name in print. That done, you can move on to the third, final, and probably most enjoyable tab:

Kindle eBook Pricing

Your first option is **KDP Select Enrollment**, which Amazon celebrates for reasons of its own, and which I think you should ignore. Does it "Maxmimize [Your] Royalties," as promised? Not mine, it didn't! When it was rolled out in 2011, Select paid $2 for books borrowed from the Kindle Online Lending Library (KOLL), a perk for Amazon Prime subscribers. That was a fair return, but it proved impossible to sustain when the company added Kindle Unlimited, a $9.99-a-month option whose subscribers could download as many books as they liked, as often as they liked, as long as they didn't have more than ten signed out at one time. Amazon hastily switched to a per-page model, and it kept reducing the payout, until now it averages less than half a cent a page.

When I did the math, I found that my book selling for $4.99 was valued at 70 cents under this model, and to make matters worse, I wasn't allowed to offer it through any other vendor. No thanks! I now have no books at all in KDP Select. (Funnily enough, last month I earned 22 cents from this Guide, which a KU subscriber had evidently kept handy for several years. He or she read 48 pages in December.)

Territories. In almost every case, you can and should click on **All territories (worldwide rights)**, which will put your book on sale on all Amazon stores, which at this writing include the United States, Canada, Britain, France, Germany, Netherlands, Spain, Italy, Mexico, Brazil, India, Australia, and Japan. (Residents of Ireland can shop on the UK store, and those in Austria and Switzerland on the German store. There may be other such hitchhikers, and people living in most other countries can buy the book on the US Amazon store, paying a surcharge to cover taxes and delivery costs.)

Royalty and Pricing. There's an option here to compare your book with similar titles. The theory is that, at a lower price, you will sell more copies, and hopefully earn more money. The prompting isn't bad, though I often choose a somewhat higher price and have never regretted doing so.

I strongly suggest that you choose the **70 percent royalty** and (as a necessary condition) price your book between $2.99 and $9.99, probably at the lower end of the range. Too many self-published books are "deplorably awful," in the words of one poster on the Kindle forums, and this is especially true of those selling for 99 cents and $1.99 or borrowed through Kindle Unlimited, with the result that some of us steer clear of such titles. KDP Select also has a so-called "promotion" option, whereby a book can be offered free for up to five days in a 90-day period. This may have been a good idea when it was first introduced, but it has since been cheapened by a flood of badly written and badly formatted books. Now, when the sophisticated shopper sees a "freebie" — or a book priced at 99 cents or even $1.99 — his or her first reaction is often to move on to something more desirable. For that reason, and for the sake of the 70 percent royalty, I price even my shortest e-books at $2.99, and most of them for more, topping out at $5.95.

Immediately following my selection of the 70 percent royalty for this Guide, I see a line that reads:

Your book file size after conversion is 0.99 MB

This information is as important as it is inconspicuous. The 70 percent royalty is reduced by a **download fee** of 15 cents per megabyte — one reason why it's important to upload clean html rather than the mess turned out by a word processor. From the retail price of $3.49, Amazon subtracts 15 cents for the bother and expense of delivering my Guide to the customer, and pays me 70 percent of the balance, which comes to $2.34. That's an actual return of 67 percent.

These are US dollar prices and apply to the **Primary Marketplace**, which is the US Amazon store, where digital self-publishing got its start. But don't overlook those **Other Marketplaces!** Click on that link and a new field opens up, with twelve markets including Britain (the most important, in my experience) and the five euro stores. You can let your US price convert automatically to other currencies, or you can specify a price for each. I think you should do the latter. The price you enter is "VAT inclusive," meaning that it is you who pays the sales tax. This Guide, priced at $3.49 in the United States, goes for £2.95 in Britain and €3.49 in France, Germany, Netherlands, Italy, and Spain. At current exchange rates and VAT charges, I earn about the same in Europe as I do at home.

Tax is also included in the price you set for the stores in India, Japan, and Australia. Elsewhere, the price I enter will be what my royalty is based on, so all I have to think about is the exchange rate and the general price level in the target country. (I lowball the price for India, Mexico, and Brazil. I try, however, to have them end in the figure 95, which I prefer to the more traditional 99.)

Book Lending. If you have opted for the 70 percent royalty, you cannot opt out of lending. But even if, for reasons of your own, you want to price your book below $2.99 or more than $9.99, I think that the possibility of a one-time loan of the book to a friend of the buyer is a fine idea, and I often loan my e-books, just as I do with print editions. (Indeed, I sometimes wish I could loan a book more than just the one time.) Note that this lending option has nothing to do with the borrows that are part of KDP Select and Kindle Prime, in which you receive a small fee for each page read.

~ ~ ~ ~

You are now ready to publish, but don't be in a hurry! Click the button that says **Save as Draft**. Make at least one final review before you **Save and Publish**. Once you do that, there is no turning back. Unless the auto-mated review finds something amiss in your book, it will be available for purchase on the Amazon store within 24 hours, often the same day.

Incidentally, the first two tabs will show as *Complete*, but the Kindle eBook Pricing tab may be tagged as *in Progress*. If you have successfully published your book, don't worry about it. That's just the way it is.

The Other E-tailers

For several years, I distributed my books through **Smashwords** to give them additional exposure, but I turned against the platform for four reasons. First, the formatting from the Smashwords "Meatgrinder" struck me as bad, to be charitable. Second, Smashwords didn't offer DRM, meaning that my books became open to infinite circulation by the first person to download a copy. Third, I found it impossible to control my pricing, because some of Smashwords's outlets discounted aggressively. Amazon would match the discounted price, which not only reduced my income from the book but sometimes halved it by throwing me into the 35 percent royalty. Finally, I didn't like the long delay before the money trickled in. So I bailed out of Smashwords in favor of publishing directly or indirectly to every platform I could reach by my own efforts.

I am told that Smashwords now prohibits its retailers from discounting. Furthermore, it has begun to accept the epub format, so it may be worth another look.

A more recent (and more agreeable) "aggregator" is **Draft2Digital**, which will also sell your book through most online stores and subscription services. Some years ago I uploaded an experimental book to D2D, and I was delighted with the speed it went live on Barnes & Noble, Apple, and Kobo. Draft2Digital takes 10 percent of your earnings off the top, but on the other hand you have to upload a book file and a product image only the one time, and the same is true of the book description and metadata. That struck me as a fair exchange, and I have now deleted all my books from most of the competing platforms and instead let D2D list the books, collect the royalties, and — an important consideration — send me the 1099-MISC tax form after the year ends.

D2D offers a DRM option, which I like, though it does not apply to all its retail outlets. And neither it nor Smashwords distributes books through Google Play, so I maintain my own account there. I also have an account with **Lulu**, which unlike most aggregators will market PDFs to the public.

In addition to the three principal competitors to Amazon — more about them below — D2D also distributes to the **Scribd** subscription service, to several booksellers I'd never heard of, and to **Overdrive**, which supplies e-books to libraries. I price all my books at $9.95 or $12.95 for libraries, and I have indeed sold a few. I see that one novel, published many years ago by Doubleday, is available at 27 libraries in Massachusetts alone. That's a nice feeling.

Kobo

Kobo began as a Canadian company but was acquired by Rakuten in Japan, and it sells e-books in both those countries and around the world, including on Walmart's online store. It used to be my fourth-best market, but more recently it moved into second place behind Amazon. A particularly nice feature of the Kobo platform is a world map, on which you will be rewarded with a handsome blue circle upon each country represented among your buyers. I loved that map!

Kobo's publishing platform is called **Writing Life**. Once you have set up an account, it's very straightforward — easier to understand, indeed, than the KDP platform. Go to **eBOOKS** > **Create new eBook** to begin. I twice managed to publish duplicate editions of the same book. I don't know how I did that, but it's something to watch out for. I also managed to set my preferred currency as Australian dollars; it took an email to Support to straighten that out.

Kobo requires an ISBN but will supply one at no cost. The payout is 70 percent for books priced at $2.99 or more, reduced to 45 percent for those priced below that figure. It has its own subscription service, called Kobo Plus, with a different payment system. It also has a minimum payout of $50, but I believe will pay every year even if you don't earn the minimum. Payment can be made by electronic transfer (US, Canadian, Australian, New Zealand, and Hong Kong dollars; and euros, pounds sterling, and Japanese yen). However, I now rely on Draft2Digital to upload my books to Kobo and manage the income and tax records.

Apple

When the iPad was launched in 2011, we all believed that Apple's online store would soon overtake Amazon in e-book sales. Didn't work out that way! Nevertheless, I find that my Apple royalties usually exceed those from Barnes & Noble, which at one time was second only to Amazon in digital sales. This is especially likely when US e-book sales are down, as can happen during a close-fought spectacle like the Superbowl or a presidential election. Apple has a strong presence overseas, and in countries not otherwise served by an online bookstore (Poland, South Africa, Scandinavia). This helps balance out the swings in US sales.

It's possible to upload directly to Apple, if you own a Mac computer of fairly recent vintage. I don't, and indeed I shy away from the closed Apple mini-verse, apart from my beloved iPhone 4, now eight years old and recently equipped with a new battery. That being the case, I can't advise you on the process. I have always relied on an aggregator like Draft2Digital to market my books on the iBooks Store. Apple also has an **iBooks Author** app to "create and publish" e-books, and you can feed an epub to it for the iBooks Store, but I urge you not to build your book with with the app, because it will be useless anywhere else.

Unlike other e-book retailers, Apple requires that your book must pass Epubcheck, the sub-title has to appear on the cover, and the price must end in .99.

Barnes & Noble Press

The platform most similar to Kindle Direct Publishing is Barnes & Noble Press, formerly called Nook Press. The terms are also similar, and a bit more favorable to the author. (For prices above $9.99, for example, the royalty is 65% rather than Amazon's paltry 35%.) Though once limited to the US, B&N Press now also serves authors from the UK, Ireland, Canada, Australia, New Zealand, France, Germany, Spain, Netherlands, and Belgium.

Some authors report that they sell more e-books on B&N than on Amazon. For me, there's no comparison, but so what? If you have an epub, it takes only minutes to upload it to the B&N Press platform, and you can use the same product image and most of the same marketing material. The online preview is reasonably good, and you can download the converted book to view on your computer. You might also buy a Nook, though they're pricier than Kindles, to see how your book actually looks on the device.

Like the KDP platform, B&N Press also offers a print option. More about that in my final chapter.

Google Play

There are other, smaller online bookstores and lending libraries, but to my knowledge we can't distribute through them except through a third-party aggregator like Smashwords or Draft2Digital. The exception is the awfully named **Google Play**, which I avoided for a long time because the uploading process is complicated, sales were low, and discounting was a perennial problem. Google used to discount everything by 20 percent or more. Happily, the company stopped doing this last year.

Alas, Google claims not to be accepting new sign-ups. It promises to be back soon, but that promise has been there for quite a while now. It's worth checking, though, because like Kobo and the lesser e-tailers, it serves as an anchor to windward, and small sums add up over the course of a year. Besides, monopolies make me nervous, and we are all better served with the widest possible market for our wares.

Some self-publishers have reported success in setting up a new Google account just by repeatedly asking to join. And there is at least one aggregator that distributes books through Google Play, the Italian company called **StreetLib**. It has been around for a while, and though its web interface can be difficult to negotiate — probably because its developers aren't native English speakers — I did try it out, and it has sold a few books for me through online bookstores I've never otherwise heard of.

If you do succeed in signing up with Google, you'll find that the interface is very different from the KDP and elsewhere. You'll need an epub, of course, and a product image (cover); that, and a bit of patience, should see you through.

Other Formats

Everything I've written above assumes that you are publishing in your native language, and that your native language is English. But why would you stop there? Why not make it available in **translation**? No, Amazon won't turn your prose into French, Spanish, German, or Chinese. And no, Google Translate won't do the job for you, either. (Just paste a few pages from your book into the Google Translate window. Let them migrate to Chinese or even French, then paste that version into the window and ask for it to be rendered into English again. When you stop laughing, you will understand why a robot can't do this for you.) And finally, no, you can't afford to hire a qualified translator!

There is a way around this. A company called **Babelcube** will match you up with a translator who will do the work for a share of the royalties. (At first, the split favors the translator, then as more books are sold it becomes 50/50, and finally it favors the author.) I've done one book through Babelcube, into Portuguese and Italian, finding that it was a lot more work than I had expected, and for less reward. What both translators did was upload a badly formatted Word doc, which I had to devote many hours to repairing. And Babelcube was slow to distribute the translations to online stores (especially, alas, to Amazon). As a result, I haven't yet earned the $10 minimum payment. By contrast, I not long ago got a $1800 payment from HarperCollins for a Chinese translation that didn't require anything of me.

I find that **audio books** are more profitable. Amazon has a division — **ACX**, short for Audiobook Creation Exchange — that will link you up with a professional narrator for an arranged fee or a split of the royalties. I was lucky enough to find a very good Chicago radio announcer to do the work on a 50/50 basis. It was the same short book as the one I put up for translation, and like that project it proved to be more laborious than I had expected. It does however provide a regular though small income stream. I plan to do more of this! The more anchors you set to windward, the more likely you are to weather any storm, and I wouldn't be surprised if audio becomes as profitable as digital publishing in a very few years.

Finally, of course, there is the intriguing format that Herr Gutenberg introduced more than 700 years ago. A **print edition** is so important to the success of your publishing project that I have added a chapter to this Guide to show you how it's done.

Plan B: The Ultimate Basic Framework

USING HTML TO BUILD an epub has become second nature to me, and I hope I have convinced you that the learning curve is gentle enough for anyone to surmount. But if after reading this Guide you still find the process daunting, I now fulfill my promise to provide you with Plan B, the Ultimate Basic Framework. Like all my frameworks, it is posted on my blog so you can simply copy it for your own use. You will find it at Notjohn's KDP Guide on Blogspot.

Plan B will suffice for simple books to be sold through Kindle Direct Publishing. It has no illustrations, though you could certainly tweak it to include them; and it is meant to be uploaded directly to the KDP, though you could run it through Sigil to make an epub for other retailers. I've trimmed the style sheet to the essentials and put it at the beginning of the html file. In short, Plan B is very like what I used to upload to the Amazon store for three years, 2009-2011, after I stopped relying on Word but before I discovered the marvels of epub. It starts like this:

```
<?xml version="1.0" encoding="utf-8"?>
<!DOCTYPE html PUBLIC "-//W3C//DTD
XHTML 1.1//EN"
"http://www.w3.org/TR/xhtml11/DTD/xhtml11.dtd">
<html
xmlns="http://www.w3.org/1999/xhtml">
<head>
```

<title>Your Book Title Goes Here</title>
<!--First we have a basic style sheet, sufficient to format our book-->

The first four entries, up to and including **<head>** are necessary boilerplate. You can ignore them. In the next line, replace *"Your Book Title Goes Here"* with — the title of your book! Leave the opening and closing title tags just as they are.

The next item is a **comment**. In an html file, anything enclosed by **<!--** and **-->** will be ignored when the file is displayed on a screen, whether it be a computer monitor, a Kindle, or a smartphone. You can leave such comments in the html file, because they won't be visible in the final book. Or remove them, if you like to be neat.

The style sheet

The style sheet that follows is a much-simplified version of the **epub.css** described in Step 2. You can of course add any elements from that larger style sheet, but here are the styles most likely to be needed:

<style type="text/css">
p { margin-top:0.0em; margin-bottom:0.0em; text-indent:1.5em; text-align:justify; }
p.first { margin-top:0.5em; margin-bottom: 0.0em; text-indent:0.0em; text-align:justify; }
p.center { margin-top:0.0em; margin-bottom:0.25em; text-indent:0.0em; text-align:center; }
h2 { margin-top:1em; font-size: 150%; text-indent: 0em; text-align:center; }
p.large { font-weight: bold; margin-top:1em; font-size: 200%; text-indent: 0em; text-align:center; }

```
p.medium { margin-top:1em; font-weight:
bold; font-size: 150%; margin-top:1.0em; text-
indent: 0em; text-align:center; }
p.small { font-weight: bold; margin-top:1em;
font-size: 125%; text-indent: 0em; text-
align:center; }
</style>
</head>
<body>
```

Okay. You have now finished the *head* of your book and are ready to begin the *body* section, starting with the title page.

The title page

Following the *body* tag, Plan B continues like this:

```
<!--Next we have a title page with each line
centered-->
<p class="large" id="start">Your Book
Title</p>
<p class="medium">The Subtitle</p>
<p class="small">Author</p>
<p class="small">Publisher <a href="#copy">
2020 </a></p>
```

As before, you can ignore the comment while substituting your book title, subtitle, and author and publisher names in place of my text. That hotlink to **#copy** will carry the interested reader (there won't be many) to the copyright statement at the back of the book. To see how this works in practice, go to my Table of Contents and click on the last entry. For the html of a typical copyright page you can adapt, go to Step 7.

If you have made the transition to Sigil, you can use its TOC tool instead of laying down these hotlinks.

The table of contents

```
<!--Which is followed by the Table of Contents,
also centered-->
<mbp:pagebreak />
<h2 id="toc">Contents</h2>
<p class="center">1 - <a href="#chapter01">
Chapter One </a></p>
<p class="center">2 - <a href="#chapter02">
Chapter Two </a></p>
<p class="center">3 - <a href="#chapter03">
Chapter Three </a></p>
<p class="center"><a href="#copy">
Copyright </a></p>
```

Again, you can ignore the comment or remove it. It is followed by a tag you have not seen before, and which is unique to the Kindle platform: **mbp:pagebreak**. This is a shortcut for forcing a chapter or other major section onto a new page in a Kindle e-book, and it harks back to Kindle's beginning in the Mobipocket software. (Here too, Sigil's more sophisticated workflow eliminates the need for this marker, which does not work in the epub format.) So your TOC will not follow directly below your publisher name, except perhaps on the Look Inside sample on the Amazon store. The reader will have to "turn" to the next e-book page, just as he or she would do in a print edition.

The framework then provides three chapters plus a link to the copyright page. You can of course create as many additional chapters as you like, and if you prefer to give the links actual names instead of calling them **chapter04** and so on, you can do that, too. (Note that the number sign — # — is necessary and has a particular meaning in an html file. It instructs the software to look for the associated anchor *within the same document*, rather than in another file or on the World Wide Web. If you upload a Plan B file to the KDP platform, it will consist of just the one, fairly long file.)

Chapter by chapter

In Step 5, I explained how to transform a Word document into a reliable html file by running it through the utility at **Word2CleanHtml.com** online, or by using a purpose-built software or plug-in. You'll want to do the same thing here. But for Plan B, you should modify that system a bit. Either break your document into chapters, clean them, and paste them one at a time into the framework. Or create a separate text or html file containing the entire book, then copy and paste the chapters to the framework as you proceed through it.

<!--And now the text chapters, as many as you like-->
<mbp:pagebreak />
<h2 id="chapter01">Chapter One</h2>
<p class="first">
<!--The first paragraph in a chapter should be flush left, perhaps with a few words capitalized-->
</p>
<p>
<!--Each following paragraph should be indented, and each should end with a closing tag, as shown below-->
</p>

I assume you will have a more dramatic title than "Chapter One," so you will substitute that for my plain-vanilla version. (And note that if you have changed the links in the TOC, you must correspondingly change the anchors here. So if your chapter title is "Girl Meets Boy," you might have made the link read **#girl**, so you'll want to change the anchor here to **id="girl"**.)

I then call for a first paragraph that is flush to the left margin, and I suggest that you capitalize the first several words as I have done throughout this Guide. This paragraph tag — **<p class="first">** — should replace the first **<p>** in the markup provided by the clean-up software.

But if messing about with the html makes you nervous, well, go ahead and let your chapters begin with an indented first paragraph. You can do this by deleting everything following the chapter title. In any case, you'll want to do just that with what follows the first paragraph, because the clean markup contains all the opening and closing tags that you will require. The simplified framework will then look like this:

```
<mbp:pagebreak />
<h2 id="chapter01">Chapter One</h2>
<!--Insert the clean markup for Chapter One here-->
```

Finishing the book

Subsequent chapters are added just as the first one was, and the book is finished off as follows:

```
<!--Adapt for as many chapters as you have, then end with the copyright-->
<mbp:pagebreak />
<h2 id="copy">Copyright</h2>
<p class="first"> </p>
</body>
</html>
```

Which of course is just another chapter, plus the tags that close off the body of the book and the html file as a whole.

If you are working in Notepad++ as I recommended in Step 1, the html tags will be displayed in colors that signal whether they are correct. (Sigil's Code View also color-codes the html, though the hues are less dramatic.) You can also Tidy and Prettify the html by running it through **infohound.net/tidy** online.

One caution: if you use Word2CleanHtml as I do, you may find that it sometimes inserts a blank and useless web address, which might look something like this: *<a name="_wsQP_"></a>*. You probably should delete any of these that you find, because any e-tailer that runs books through **Epubcheck** will refuse it as invalid formatting. At present, only Apple does this, but others may follow in the future, so it's a good habit to cultivate.

You may now upload your Html file to Kindle Direct Publishing. The conversion and previewing will be exactly as described in Step 10 above.

And now your work is done — congratulations! And I hope you have found Plan B so easy that next time you'll go the full epub route, at which point the whole bright world of e-publishing will be open to you.

Purpose-built Software

S URE, YOU CAN FORGET all that "html stuff" and buy a software package that claims to simplify the whole process. The promise is that you can go from finished book (or even a first draft!) and turn it into a properly formatted mobi file for Amazon or epub for the other retailers. I hasten to add that *I don't think you should do this.* Perhaps that's only because I've spent so much time and effort learning how to work with html and epub, but I don't think so. I want to control what goes on in the background, rather than leave it to a programmer I've never met. But if you are looking for a shortcut, here are your options:

Scrivener

Scrivener is a full-fledged word processor, in which you can build your book from first draft to final draft and on through the formatting process. It's even equipped with a "corkboard" where you can enter your research notes or early-morning thoughts, then access them later to incorporate into your book. At the end of the process, you can export the finished book as html, a PDF, an epub, or a "mobi" tailored to the Amazon Kindle. Thus, if you have a reviewer in mind, you can provide a PDF that anyone can read on a computer (and on some e-book devices). And the PDF of course would come in handy when it's time to publish your book in paperback.

Scrivener costs $49 for Windows or Apple computers, and there's a 30-day trial version. Get it at Literature and Latte dot com. There is a lengthy Scrivener

Boot Camp seminar on YouTube that you might find useful, though it's now six years old.

Jutoh

Jutoh is probably the most-used e-book formatting software. It too has a text editor, but I suspect that most users have already written their e-book on Word or another word processor. The software works on Windows, Mac, and Linux, and sells for $45. (There's an $90 version intended for publishers of multiple titles. I have no idea what advantages this version has, if any.) You can download the software without paying for it. This gives you a somewhat limited trial version, which you can later upgrade to one that enables you to publish the formatted book.

The website at **Jutoh.com** has video tutorials and a link to a 200-page operator's manual. One caution: the website boasts that "We talk to you," but I have heard more than one customer complain that the developer takes very badly to criticism. So if you do "talk to him," you might want to grovel a bit. (In fact, this is very good advice any time you are posting on a technical forum. Programmers and saints have a very different DNA.)

At least one author-publisher swears by Jutoh for salvaging books written in Apple Pages. He saves the Pages word-processing file as an epub, opens that epub in Jutoh, adds the cover, saves it again as an epub, and uploads it to the various online distributors.

Atlantis Word Processor

Like Scrivener, AWP purports to be a full-fledged word processor (hence its title), suitable for writing a book from the git-go. For my part, I just imported an already-written book from Word. I saved it as an epub without further ado; then I opened the epub in Sigil to see how it had fared. I was impressed by the squeaky-clean html, but less so by the way it interpreted my paragraphs. All were flush left, which in my opinion isn't acceptable, though I easily fixed them by importing my own style sheet and substituting it for the one created by AWP. I'm told that my mistake was in not spending enough time with the program, to specify my desired indents. Indeed, a formatter whom I admire tells me that Atlantis is by far the best of the purpose-built tools for making e-books.

The software is available for all Windows versions dating back to XP (which is no longer supported by Microsoft, and thus is no longer safe to use on the internet). The 30-day trial period gives you a full-featured program, though the book is watermarked to discourage you from publishing without registering the software, which costs $35 (or $49 for free future up-dates). AWP is available in multiple languages and with a spell checker at **AtlantisWordProcessor.com**.

Calibre

Calibre is a magnificent library management tool. I use it a lot. I particularly appreciate that it enables me to con-vert a mobi file to an epub, or vice versa, so that I'm not left looking at a blank screen because I downloaded the wrong format. (I am told that its proper name is "calibre" — no caps! — but I find that annoying, so I capitalize the first letter here and in what follows.)

Calibre is free, and it will open a Word doc, and for that reason some self-publishers use it to create Kindle editions. I don't think this is a good idea. The software simply is not designed for that purpose; it creates style classes that to me seem unintelligible; and Amazon used to reject Calibre-generated mobi files without any apparent reason. This no longer seems to be the case, but why take the risk when Sigil is so much better at this task?

You can download the software (and make a donation, if you like) at **Calibre-Ebook.Com**. There are versions for Windows, Mac OS, and Linux, and there's a busy and excellent Calibre forum at **MobileRead.Com** (look under E-Book Software.) I am a great fan of these forums, and I visit them often, though mostly for help with any Sigil problems I encounter. It's especially comforting that the developers – both for Calibre and for Sigil – are regular contributors there.

A few years ago, Sigil's then-developer abandoned the software in hopes that someone else would come along to continue the good work, which did soon happen. In the meantime, Kovid Goyal adapted Calibre for the express purpose of creating e-books, rather than just managing them for one's personal library. I have never used **Calibre Companion**, but if you are hooked on the basic library management tool, you might give it a try. There's a sub-forum at MobileRead for the Companion software.

Writer2ePub

OpenOffice and LibreOffice are free, open-source suites that compete directly with Microsoft Office, including its famous word processor. I have long used OpenOffice Writer and for some purposes prefer it to Word. (Others favor LibreOffice, which is more regularly updated.) The Italian programmer Luke Calcinai created a plug-in that works with either of these free software programs, and also with NeoOffice. Get it at **Writer2Epub.It**.

When I downloaded the plug-in, it installed itself, after asking my permission, and added a small menu at the left of the OpenOffice toolbar. I clicked on the first, green icon, opened a book-length OOW file, and was presented with a "metadata" screen where I could enter the title, author, publisher, and so on, even to the book's description. Since my object was only to see how neat a job Signor Calcinai had done, I skipped most of this and saved the document as an epub, which I then opened in Sigil. The html was very clean, though here too I had lost much of my formatting, with the chapter heads simply boldfaced and centered on the page. I'd want to do quite a bit of clean-up in Sigil, adding my own style sheet and so on. But Writer2ePub certainly gave me something to work with, and presumably much of this clean-up can be done in OOW itself before exporting to epub format.

Since OpenOffice is available for Mac operating systems, Writer2ePub might offer a way out for Mac users who can't otherwise find an economical tool for creating an e-book.

Vellum

The most expensive purpose-built software for e-book publishers is Vellum, which is for Apple computers only, and like so many things in the Apple-verse is outrageously priced. It sells for an eye-watering $199.99 for e-books only, or $249.99 if you also want to publish print editions, as of course you should. That's getting up into Microsoft territory! It's a free download, however, so you can try it out to see if you like it; get it at **Vellum.Pub**. Weirdly, you must download the software before you can actually purchase it.

I love my iPhone 4, which still runs beautifully at six years of age, but I detest the closed Apple-verse and the way the company obsoletes its hardware at regular intervals. So I have no way of testing Vellum myself, but those who have tried it are near-delirious in their enthusiasm. Indeed, to read some of the online discussions about the software on Kboards Writers Cafe is to wonder if you've been wafted to California and enrolled in its latest cult.

In addition to an Apple operating system, you must have a word processor capable of saving in **.docx** format: Microsoft Word, LibreOffice Writer, Apple's own Pages, or (and this seems odd, since it's a competitor) Scrivener. The free, online Google Docs also saves as docx, though I haven't been able to find anyone who has used it successfully with Vellum.

Since Vellum is free to download, you can actually format a book before deciding whether or not to buy the software. There is a fixed number of "themes" or styles, meaning that your book will look like a lot of others. In some of the samples I've seen, the initial drop-cap looks fine in the online sample on the Amazon store but fails in the purchased book when viewed on the Kindle Paperwhite, unless the reader turns on **Publisher Fonts**. (It's not a bad fail, and I wouldn't rule out Vellum for that reason alone.) Finally, I'm told that the software cannot provide internal hotlinks, as I have done repeatedly in the digital edition of this Guide, though you *can* link to an external website.

However, Vellum is notorious for creating bloated html — the worst software by far, I'm told. This means you pay a 15-cent-per-megabyte penalty if you choose the 70 percent option on the KDP platform.

Kindle Create

A few years ago, Amazon introduced what was clearly intended as a Vellum-killer. And like the company's other self-publishing tools, it was free! Kindle Create has so far gone through three stages: as an online app, as a plug-in for Word, and now as a standalone software that you can download to your PC (Windows 7 onward) or Apple computer (OS 10.9 or later). What's more, like Vellum, it can now build a print edition.

KC doesn't have nearly as many fans as Vellum, but at least one formatter thinks it's great stuff, at least for people willing to "play with it and practice, practice, practice," in his words. (Which raises the question: why not simply do the same with Microsoft Word or another word processor — or better yet, with Sigil?) Amazon's KC help page is hard to find and really not all that helpful. Go to the KDP platform on Amazon.com and search for Kindle Create, which should bring up a page offering three guides, of which only the first, *Prepare Reflowable Books*, is of much interest to me. As explained elsewhere, I have little interest in fixed-format e-books, and I recommend staying away from them.

KC has just four "themes" or templates: **Classic**, for fiction and non-fiction; **Cosmos**, for sci-fi or dystopian fiction; **Modern**, for I don't know what, and **Amour**, for (what else?) romance. I found myself choosing Classic as an all-purpose layout, perhaps with Modern as an alternative for a how-to manual like this one. The software offers formatting tools that would take some effort to learn in html — drop caps, for example.

Like most of the tools Amazon provides for self-publishers, the "kpf" file turned out by Kindle Create works only on the Amazon store. (This isn't true of the print edition.) For me, that's a fatal lack, so I'll never use it. The software's apostle scoffs at this concern: all one needs do, he points out, is build an epub for the other online stores. But why would anyone do that? If you can make an epub, you're good to go on every platform, Amazon included. Why build two e-books when one is all you need?

Still, Kindle Create is certainly worth keeping an eye on. It has come a long way in just two years, and perhaps Amazon will eventually build a version that can be uploaded to the Apple, Kobo, Barnes & Noble, and other online stores. Then, like Vellum, it might serve as a lazy author's way into the reader's shopping cart, and without the high price of admission.

Draft to Digital

And in fact there is just such an automagical converter available to us. Draft to Digital, the "aggregator" I recommended earlier, offers a quasi-Vellum tool that, like Kindle Create, is free to all comers. Sign in to your D2D account, complete the first tab in the publishing process, upload the novel as a more or less complete Word document, fill out the book details, and go to the **Preview** stage. Here, you see your book laid out in the default (*D2D Simple*) format. On the right side of the screen, you are invited to **Choose a Style**. There are six "All-Purpose" styles including *D2D Simple*, four "*Mystery and Thriller*" styles, three "*Romance*," and so on, for a grand total of seventeen options including two for non-fiction. Alas, you can't preview them online: you must download the various formats (mobi for Amazon, epub for the rest of the digital world, pdf for a print edition) and preview them on your computer.

The result isn't bad, though you'll probably find, as I did, that you must go back to your original Word doc and do quite a bit of touch-up. And you may want to play around with a few other styles before settling on one that satisfies you. Note that there's no requirement that you actually distribute the book through D2D, though almost certainly you will do that for the epub. But you can take the mobi file and publish it through KDP, and you can take the pdf and run it through KDP Print, IngramSpark, or Barnes & Noble Press.

I was mostly interested in the print edition. It wasn't bad! The front matter was a disaster, but that was because there wasn't any in my manuscript. The software did a fair job with the title page, an unimpressive job with the copyright page, and left the table of contents blank. But chapter one began (as it should) on a right-hand page, paginated with an Arabic numeral 1 centered at the bottom, with subsequent pages paginated in the header, which also included my name as author on all verso (left-hand) pages and the book's title on the facing page. There was little hyphenation, but most of that was acceptable — better than the automagical hyphenation in our Kindle e-books. I thought the curlicues showing breaks in the narrative were oversized and ugly, but that was probably my fault for choosing a romantic theme.

~ ~ ~ ~

I played about with all of these purpose-built programs except Vellum (which as a Windows user I can't access without more trouble than it seems to be worth). Like Word, any one of them can indeed create a reasonable e-book — perhaps better than Word, in some cases. But I wouldn't trust them to do the job. Instead, I would simply save as epub, open the epub in Sigil, and finish it there. That being the case, I just don't see the point, at least not in the foreseeable future. Your mileage, of course, may differ.

When it comes to the print edition, I think that Draft2Digital's online converter shows real promise. I take enough pride in my books, however, that for now I'll continue to format them myself, as I explain in the final chapter.

How To Kindle a Fire

I COULDN'T RESIST the pun in the title of this chapter, and I apologize if I've led you astray. This isn't about marketing your book but about making it the best and most successful book you can possibly produce. Or — to phrase it differently — if I couldn't find a place for an idea in the earlier chapters, I've put it here.

While Building Your Book

A publisher's toolkit

Here are three books every author-publisher should own and use:

The Chicago Manual of Style: There have been seventeen editions of this essential resource, the most recent in 2017. I gave it to my editor-wife for Christmas, then borrowed it back, but I would be perfectly happy using our copy of the 14th Edition from 1993. And here's the good news: while the current *Manual* lists for $70 and is discounted to $43.33 this morning at a popular online bookstore, you can usually buy a secondhand copy of the 14th, 15th, or 16th Edition for $5 or $10 including postage. Any one will serve. The rules don't change very fast.

Webster's Collegiate Dictionary: There is no end to the uses of a good dictionary, and no online version comes close to this basic reference, which I have owned in one edition or another since high school. I use it mostly as a check on American spelling and usage. Indeed, I opened it just this morning to see if "à la carte" should be italicized. (No, because the phrase is included in the main body of the dictionary, not under Foreign Words and Phrases.) When it comes to the more serious task of defining words and understanding where they came from, I turn to **The Shorter Oxford English Dictionary**. Like the *Chicago Manual*, it's pricey if bought new but quite a bargain (I see several copies at $10 or so, including shipping) if you settle for the older, handsome, two-volume set from 1993. Again, definitions don't change very fast.

The Elements of Style: Originally a pamphlet by William Strunk of Cornell University, this handbook was updated by his student E B White, and that version has since been updated by White's stepson, Roger Angell. In whatever edition, it is a priceless asset for any writer, from high school to old age. The 4th Edition from 1999 lists for $9.95 in paperback but is often discounted to less than half that, and sometimes you can find used copies for a penny plus shipping. An even better bargain is Professor Strunk's original, as published in 1920: it's free at the Gutenberg Project website and also in a Kindle edition.

If you live elsewhere, you may object that most of my reference books are products of the United States. But ask yourself: what store sells the vast majority of our e-books? It's Amazon's US store. You may be accustomed to single quotes rather than double quotes, and to seeing *colour* rather than *color*, but you should be aware that Americans don't share your preference, especially since it's we who are the insular people. We still use "English" measure for most purposes, while the British have pretty much gone over to metric. More shameful still, most of us have read the Harry Potter books in American translation.

Hiring it done

My wife and daughter will testify that I am one of the world's most tight-fisted men. As a child of the Great Depression, I hate to spend money. But I early learned that my notion of a handsome e-book cover left something to be desired, and that I could do better, both artistically and financially, if I paid someone else to do this work. I have paid as little as $6 and as much as $140, the first for a cover from India by way of Fiverr, the second from a pro in Massachusetts. You can of course pay $1000 or more for a professional design, but my Yankee thrift has never allowed me to go there. Nor do I think the investment would ever pay off.

I don't spend anything for editing. But I worked as a copywriter and editor for several years, I married a young woman with a similar background (we met at the publications office when I took a leave of absence and Susan interviewed for my job), and we have earned our living ever since as free-lance writers and editors, sometimes one and sometimes the other. So I have invested the fabled 10,000 hours required to master any craft, whether editing a book for HarperCollins or playing the piano at Carnegie Hall. Have you?

Fifty years ago, when the vast majority of books were published by a handful of prestigious firms in New York, London, and other centers of commerce and culture, a writer didn't need to know about editing, copy-editing, or proof-reading. (Which are, by the way, three different tasks.) There were editors on staff to worry about the organization and content of the book, a stable of free-lancers to make sure words were spelled correctly and sentences obeyed good English usage, and proof-readers to ensure that no mistakes were made in translating the manuscript into print. There are no such gatekeepers for your book. At the very least, think about hiring a copy-editor (or about marrying one, as I did). *We don't know what we don't know.* I once wrote a 140,000-word book about aviation, in which I spelled *hangar* as if airplanes were stored on coat-hangers. The publisher's copy-editor quietly corrected the mistake, probably fifty or sixty times. What if there had been no copy-editor between me and publication?

Every Saturday, I look at the best-seller list in the *Wall Street Journal*, searching for self-published books. Nearly every week there's a novel by an indie author, and once in a while there are two. (And one Saturday last December, there were three!) Almost every one of those best-sellers shares three characteristics: the cover was designed by a professional; the text was edited by a professional; and the e-book was formatted by a professional. Learn from that — but don't give up in despair. In the winter of 2015-16 there was also an indie on the non-fiction list, *Maude*, by Donna Mabry. It's a lovely book, and Ms Mabry tells me that it was formatted as a Word doc by her daughter.

Most of those best-sellers shared two other characteristics: they were available in paperback, and in addition to Amazon they were sold by online booksellers like Apple, Kobo, and Barnes & Noble. Which is another way of saying *they weren't enrolled in Kindle Select*. You will never be a best-selling author if you limit yourself to Amazon.

Embedded fonts

As with your plans for a striking cover, so it is with your appetite for far-out typefaces: your taste is not shared by everyone, and probably not by a majority of readers. My rule on such matters is: *let the defaults rule!* Don't try to override the platform's preferred display. There are several reasons for this. In the first place, you must have the technical knowledge to embed fonts, and you must have the right to do so. Just because a font is on your computer does not mean it is free for you to distribute to the rest of the world.

Second, Amazon has been known to strip out the typeface instructions or the actual embedded fonts in an uploaded e-book, and the same may be true of other e-tailers. And third, if you get past the obstacles and do succeed in forcing your notion of good typography upon the world, you may annoy the purchaser by preventing him or her from setting the typeface to something else. Never forget that annoyed readers are the ones who post the one-star reviews.

None of this prevents you from using a second default typeface on Kindles and some other devices, which mostly provide for a typewriter-like display called *Courier* or *monospace*. My style sheet has several such paragraph styles. If you use them, however, I suggest you do so sparingly.

How big is your book?

Amazon charges a delivery fee for e-books, if they qualify for the 70 percent royalty — 15 cents per megabyte. You can minimize the cost by uploading a book file with few images and clean coding. One of the reasons I don't like the automagical conversions from Word, Scrivener, Vellum, and other programs is that their html tends to be complicated and therefore bulky — a Word doc, for example, will cut more deeply into your Kindle royalties than one formatted as I described in Step Five. Vellum also has a reputation for messy — hence expensive — code. An 80,000-word novel need cost no more than 10 cents per download. Twenty photographs at a thrifty 127 kilobytes will add about 40 cents to that. So, even if you price your book at the minimum of $2.99, you will still take home a royalty of $1.59. (The same book, sold on another online store and distributed by an aggregator like Draft2Digital, might return 60 percent of the retail price, or $1.79.)

The size of your Word doc or epub is not a reliable guide to the download fee, and neither is the *File size* shown on the Amazon store page. You will see the actual figure on the third (pricing) tab as you work toward publication. For example, for my largest book, with 140,000 words and twenty photographs and line drawings, I see this:

Your book file size after conversion is 2.91 MB

So the download fee was (and still remains) about 45 cents. By contrast, the Amazon store page gives a file size of 4.25 MB. And the "mobi" file that I downloaded during the publishing process? It weighed in at a scary 7.45 MB, because it contained versions of the book for both the new KF8 format and the older KF7 devices, and perhaps the new KFX format as well.

The question doesn't arise with other e-tailers, because no other online store charges a download fee.

After Publication

Author Central

Amazon provides an excellent tool in Author Central. As soon as you publish, you should set up an account and claim your book. It will show up within a day or two. You now have almost unlimited control of how your book is displayed on the Amazon store. Click on the tab that says

Books, then on the title of your book. It is the tab **Editorial Reviews** that is most important to your success.

You are first presented with the opportunity to add an actual review, assuming your book has received one. The intention here is to allow for excerpts from criticism published in magazines or newspapers, but I have found that Amazon is fairly liberal in how it interprets this, accepting any "reputable source" — web sites, blogs, and online stores (including Amazon itself). You can add several reviews, up to a maximum of 1750 characters, which Amazon helpfully defines as "5 reviews of 350 characters or about 70 words each." This is a generous policy. Take advantage of it if you can.

That is followed by **Product Description**. As the page warns you, don't paste text from a word processor; instead, use a plain-text editor like Notepad, so it won't have hidden formatting in it. You will see an option for italicizing or bolding text, and you can insert paragraphs simply by using the Enter key on your keyboard twice, though I have found that that sometimes doesn't work. Instead, I use one **
** tag for a line break, and two of them to get an empty line between paragraphs.

Unlike KDP Book Details, Author Central offers a preview option, so you can play about with the book description until you're happy with the result. (Incidentally, this little essay is not a "blurb," as so many authors seem to think. A blurb is when Stephen King writes a sentence of praise about your book, probably without ever reading it, in the expectation that you will return the favor one day.)

There are Author Central options on the US, UK, FR, DE, and JP stores. I have lived in the first four countries at one time or another, and can therefore claim some relationship to them, so I have an AC account at each of them, though I do everything in English. In theory, the Author Central book description overrides whatever description you provided on the KDP platform, though if you ever republish your book, the KDP description rules. For that reason, and also because last year the theory sometimes failed to work in practice, I now copy the html from Author Central, paste it into the KDP Book Details window, and hit Publish again.

From the Author gives you the chance to address the shopper directly. Here is a good place to explain *why* you wrote the book, what inspired you, what you hope to accomplish with it — your own story, in short.

From the Inside Flap refers to the dustcover flap on a hardcover edition, but I have used this section to publish an excerpt from the book that might appeal to a customer, but won't appear in the Look Inside or downloadable samples. (These show only the first 10 percent of the text.) The content limit here is about 1600 words, again a very generous allotment, considering that you can choose your excerpt and even abridge it if you like.

From the Back Cover again refers to a print edition, but with a bit of ingenuity you might be able to put it to use. If you have more favorable reviews than will fit in the section allotted to them, you could include some here.

Finally, there's **About the Author**. Here you can enter a short and engaging biography, stressing those aspects of your life or experience that especially bear upon the book in question. (It is here that my UK, DE, and FR pages differ from the US store.)

I'm not suggesting that you should use *all* these options. Choose the ones that best serve your purpose.

After completing your book information, you can move on to the **Profile** tab. Here again you can enter a short biography. If you have several books and have only entered an alternative biography for a few of them, this is the default version that will appear on the product page of the others. If you have an author's blog, you can add an RSS feed below the biography. (Images do not appear on Amazon's About the Author page, only the text from the blog.) You can and should upload a photograph, too, as well as videos if you have them and a Twitter link if you are into social media.

Social media

I seldom play about with **Facebook**, though I did set up a public **Page** on the platform. This is not the same as an everyday Facebook account, but the more businesslike option at **facebook.com/pages/create.** The platform has changed since I set up my Page, but I think you should choose the option **Community or Public Figure** and enter **Author** as the category. Only "friends" can see your personal Facebook page, but anyone can browse to and admire your professional Page and use it to shop for your book on Amazon.

Unfortunately, Mark Zuckerman has since decided to monetize these professional Pages. Instead of showing your posts to everyone who has "liked" your Page in the past, it only goes to some of them, unless you slip him a few dollars. I found that $5 will display it to all my Likers and to some of their friends, but now of course I am in the realm of paid advertising and its uncertain payback.

As for Twitter and Instagram and all that stuff, I'm a very poor guide. I spend very little time on social media, no doubt to my detriment. It is one of the few tools the self-publisher has to market his or her book without great expense. I have talked to author-publishers who spend *six hours a day* cultivating friends and fans online. If that comes naturally to you, by all means do it

— but leave yourself time to write, format, and publish your books!

The blog; the website; the newsletter

Yes, you probably should have a **blog**, but it is above my pay scale to advise you on how to go about creating one. I use Blogspot; it's free. Blogging doesn't come naturally to me, and I confess that I mostly use my blog not for its own sake but to spruce up my author page on the Amazon store, using the RSS feed made possible in Author Central.

I have several **websites**, all but one of them content-rich rather than a promotional place for my books. I spend many hours of my time maintaining these sites, and of course they contain banners and other marketing for my books. Every month, I send out what I hope is an interesting **newsletter** to about a thousand people who have signed up over the years. If I have a new book, of course I mention that, but the focus is on the subjects covered in my websites, including the books I read the previous month. I use a **MailChimp** sign-up form to harvest new email addresses, but I rely on my web host's provided software to actually send out the newsletter.

This costs very little, about $65 a year to the web-hosting company and about the same for five domain names. At a minimum, I think every author should have a presence on the web for his or her books, even if it's only a blog or a Facebook Page. I think it would be a wise plan to devise a unique title that works across all your chosen media — so, playing off my actual blog, I might have the website *NotJohnKDP.com*, and the same on Facebook. (These accounts don't actually exist, so don't bother looking for them.)

And here's a tip for selling your books from your blog

or website: as of this writing, Amazon has Kindle stores in thirteen countries. The DE store also serves several German-speaking countries, residents of Ireland shop at the UK store, and most of the rest of the world can shop at the US Amazon store.

How then do you direct a potential buyer to the right place? Happily, a clever Austrian has developed software to do the job for you. Just go to **BookLinker.Net** and enter the Amazon url (web address) for your book. You can then build a link that specifically suggests buying your book. (There are several options here, such as *view-book.at* or *getbook.at*, followed by a word that evokes your title.) No matter where in the world your customers may be located, if they click on such a link, they'll be directed to the store that serves their country. Every computer has an internet address that specifies its location, which information the BookLinker software uses to rout the request to where it belongs.

You can even add an **Amazon Associate** identification code, to earn a small referral fee on each sale, if you belong to Amazon's affiliate program. Since I began using it, BookLinker has been acquired by GeniusLink, which limits us to 2,000 clicks a month before requiring us to transition to a paying option. For good or bad, I'm nowhere near the cutoff.

KDP Select and the helicopter drop

In my perhaps sour opinion, the worst thing that ever happened to e-book publishing was the roll-out of **KDP Select** in the fall of 2011. Starting the following February, my sales went into a slump that stabilized only last year. Two reasons for this: First, all books grow old, and those I published in the early years generally found their audience back then. Few people need to buy a book more than once, and indeed Amazon makes that difficult to do in the case of digital editions. But there's a second and, I believe, more important reason: KDP Select brought several million new author-publishers into the system and encouraged us to race each other to the bottom. This served Amazon's purposes since authors who use KDP Select can't sell their books elsewhere, meaning that Kobo, Barnes & Noble, Apple, and Google became less formidable as competitors. The addition of **Kindle Unlimited** in 2014 made the situation worse, driving one lending library (Oyster) out of business and forcing another (Scribd) to change its business model. Less competition means more power to the dominant player, and that means less power for the individual author. Remember what I predicted in Step 10 about what happens to our earnings when the last big competitor drops out!

KDP Select also popularized the concept of the "helicopter drop," in which an author scatters books across the countryside, free for the taking. In KDP Select, this takes the form of a so-called "promotion" in which a book is free for up to five days in any 90-day period.

Authors of serial adventures can profit from these giveaways, if they entice new readers of the series. As a rule, however, very few people who download freebies ever turn around and actually pay money for an e-book. Why should they? There'll be another million desperate authors coming along next year. There are even freebie-of-the-day websites where you can link to a dozen free books, download them, read the most promising, then go back next week for another dozen. Most freebies are never read, let alone reviewed. As for remembering the author's name and shopping for another of his or her books, most readers never even see the title page because the book opens to page one, chapter one.

Then there was the "permafree" title, made possible

by Amazon's determination to be the low-price supplier. The publisher priced a book at zero on another bookseller's website, then reported it to Amazon, which then lowered its price to match. It no longer seems to work that way. Sometimes Amazon instructs the publisher to raise the price elsewhere or have the book blocked from sale. Or it simply ignores requests to price-match. And note that you can't have your book enrolled in Kindle Select for the permafree tactic to succeed.

Paid advertising

Many authors spend money to advertise their books, and this has become very tempting now that Amazon sells us the opportunity to place our "Sponsored Product" on the same page as a likely competitor. Like Kindle Select and the Kindle Unlimited subscription program, "Amazon Marketing Services" or **AMS** strikes me as a suicide pact. On the Kboards Writers Cafe one morning, I saw a post from a self-publisher who had budgeted $300 *a day* to promote a book on Amazon. So Jeff Bezos has transformed self-publishing from a system in which he paid us to one in which *we* pay *him*! (As a customer, too, I am turned off by these ads, which masquerade as legitimate search returns.)

I do very little advertising, though I run low-budget campaigns (bidding 6 cents for a Sponsored Product ad, with a $1.00 daily limit) for two of my books that seem to benefit from the exposure.

When All Else Fails

There is no shame in asking for help. Indeed, that's how I learned enough about formatting to write this Guide. The handiest forum for publishers is located at Kindle

Direct Publishing and is called, simply, **Community**. It is visited by a few knowledgeable authors, a couple of professional formatters, and a lot of people who don't know what they're talking about. The quality of their advice varies hugely, and few of them provide links to their books. Another drawback of the KDP Community, as recently remodeled, is that it consists of *eight* sub-forums, of which only one — "Formatting" — has a clearly defined purpose. The best practice is probably to ask your question there or in the "General" forum.

More sophisticated formatting advice can be found at the **MobileRead** website. Especially worth viewing are the forums dedicated to Sigil (under E-Book Software) and to Epub and Kindle Formats (under E-Book Formats). Finally, the **Kboards Writers' Cafe** is a useful place to pick the brains of your fellow indies — most of whom post links to their books, so you can easily see if you care to follow their advice. I visit all of these forums from time to time, and I learn a lot from them.

Then there are those professional formatters themselves. While they make a living by formatting books, some will also pitch in to answer questions as a favor or for a fee. (Make it clear up front that you are willing to pay for help.) Over the years I have been greatly impressed by the knowledge and kindness of Hitch at **Booknook.Biz**. Her website is worth visiting: it's a goldmine of information about the publishing process. Another friendly professional is Sarah at **Sleeping-CatBooks.Com**. Be aware, however, that a formatter is not a writer, may never have published a book of her own, and therefore doesn't understand the writing process. This can skew the advice she provides. I see this most obviously on Hitch's posts on the MobileRead forums: she approaches a book as an editor would, line by line, rather than as an organic whole.

And By All Means, a Paperback!

Y ES, YOU SHOULD HAVE a print edition of your book, assuming the spine is wide enough to display the title and your name. If your book is under 120 pages, you are getting into questionable territory, and you should ask yourself if the content is unique enough to bring another pamphlet into the world. (The minimum to have your name and the book's title on the spine is 100 pages — 50 sheets of paper! — but the text will be tiny.) Otherwise, I figure that if it's worth formatting in digital, it's worth formatting for paper.

You probably won't sell as many copies of the print edition, though it is an interesting fact that one of my better-selling paperbacks is only 72 pages, and has no title on the spine. Not only does it sell quite a few copies every month, but it sells twice as many in paper as it does in digital format. It's non-fiction, and a fairly difficult read, which may have something to do with it. (If I were to do it over, I would use a smaller page size and perhaps more generous margins, to beef it up a bit.) It's a somewhat expanded version of the thesis I wrote for my master's degree.

Whether the paperback is a commercial success or not, your e-book gains a lot of credibility if it's backed up by an actual, physical *book*. And best of all, on the Amazon store (though not elsewhere) the e-book edition will appear to be discounted. It's not really a discount, of course, but to cite another of my books, the shopper on the Kindle page will see something like this:

Print list price: ~~$14.95~~

Kindle price: $7.95
Save $7.00 (47 percent)

And who doesn't want to save seven dollars? (As it happens, that particular book is also non-fiction, and it too often sells more copies in print than it does in digital editions.)

The distributors

There once were three distributors worth considering, IngramSpark, CreateSpace, and KDP Print, with the last two being Amazon divisions. We could choose between them or — better yet — we could use Ingram and one of the Amazon options. I long dismissed KDP Print as an aggravating waste of time, but that has now changed. It's still aggravating, but unfortunately Amazon threw Create Space under the bus in the fall of 2018. As I write this in August 2020, KDP Print still hasn't fully shaken out, and indeed it may never do so, but we have to work with what we've got.

All three distributors used a similar (and sometimes the same) **Print on Demand** (POD) process, and when you opted for "Expanded Distribution" with KDP Print, all used the same distribution system to reach book-sellers outside Amazon.

CreateSpace. Like the Mobipocket software that underlay the Kindle, BookSurge was an independent platform that looked promising, so Jeff Bezos snapped it up, changed its name, and added it to his stable. It worked beautifully, and its books could be sold through "Expanded Distribution" at the Barnes & Noble website, Books-a-Million, the Book Depository (another Amazon-owned business, located in the UK, that mails books world-wide and also services Amazon stores that don't have POD facilities available), and even to bookstores and libraries. Alas, the CS option was closed down toward the end of 2018, and it won't be coming back.

IngramSpark was the alternative, and a good one because the parent organization, Ingram Content Group, is the channel through which books are ordered by American retailers, and especially your neighborhood bricks-and-mortar bookstore, if you are lucky enough to have one. Through a sibling, Lightning Source, it has access to print-on-demand (POD) facilities in the United States, Europe, and Japan.

Ingram got into the POD business as a service to small commercial publishers and authors with their own imprint, so its interface is more complicated than that of KDP Print. It also charges a setup fee of $49, though this is often waived. (You can probably find the latest promotion code on Kboards Writers Cafe.) These obstacles discouraged me from using it, as I am sure it discouraged many other self-publishers. Realistically, however, few bookstores will stock a book if it comes from an Amazon division, and some will be reluctant to special-order an Amazon product even for a customer.

Similarly, Amazon is reluctant to stock copies of IngramSpark books, unless they sell very well, which means that your book may carry the off-putting warning, "In stock but may require an extra 1-2 days to process."

KDP Print. In 2016, Amazon introduced a print option on the KDP platform. Despite having all the in-house knowledge available from the CreateSpace division, KDP Print suffered extreme growing pains during its first year and well into the second. The online platform was full of glitches, we couldn't get a physical proof copy or buy copies at a discount for our own use, and — true to Amazon's blinkered view of the book market — KDP Print books weren't available on competing stores, notably Barnes & Noble in the US and the Book Depository worldwide. (That was true also of several Amazon stores, in countries where the company lacked a POD partner.)

Most of these deficiencies were eventually made good, and KDP Print has at last become an acceptable option for printing and distributing our books. There are still occasional glitches, and the setup can be infuriating, especially for those that have images that "bleed" to the outside edge of the page.

Using both. An obvious workaround is to exploit the advantages of both companies, and some self-publishers have done just that. Design your book for IngramSpark, and publish it there first, using an International Standard Book Number (ISBN) that you own (see below). Meanwhile, adapt the book for KDP Print, where the main adjustment will be to check the thickness of the spine, which can vary because of the different paper used by the two companies. Any competent graphic artist can provide that service.

You can and should use the same ISBN in both versions. But (and this is important) don't choose Expanded Distribution for the KDP Print version. Now your book will be available for order by bookstores, libraries, and schools, and for purchase through virtually every online retailer, thanks to IngramSpark. (And your return on those sales will be much higher.) And thanks to KDP Print you'll have prompt shipping on the Amazon store, plus the ability to buy author copies at cost, which you can sell by mail or at autograph parties. And when its POD printers break down or are clogged with orders, as has happened in December 2017 and December 2018, Amazon will fill orders with the Ingram edition.

Barnes & Noble Press

Barnes & Noble has also entered the print business, and

like IngramSpark it offers both paperback and hardcover editions. Indeed, B&N's books are actually produced by Ingram's Lightning Source division. The print edition can be ordered at any B&N retail store. If your book sells 500 copies on the B&N website in a 12-month period, you can host a signing event at your local store; sell 1,000, and you can pitch it to store managers nationwide. (To be sure, selling that many copies on B&N is a very high hurdle.) The company will also promote your book through "monthly themed collections, dedicated emails to fans of your book's genre, discount alerts, and the NOOK First Look program, which gives B&N readers early access to new books every month." I assume this applies to print editions as well as to e-books.

On the downside, B&N Press does not distribute its books to other online booksellers. And I'm told that, if you have published through IngramSpark or Amazon using your own ISBN, B&N will reject it as already used. I assume but don't know that you can get around this by publishing at B&N before approaching the others.

The ISBN

And yes, you need an *International Standard Book Number* for your print edition, though you may not have obtained one for the digital version. In Canada and some other countries, ISBNs are "free" (meaning that the cost is borne by the taxpayer), but Americans buy them from the Bowker company (1 for $125, 10 for $295, 100 for $575). In the UK, they're sold by the Nielson company at roughly comparable prices (£89 for one, £369 for 100).

Amazon also offers "free" ISBNs (meaning that the company pays the up-front cost) but of course they come with a downside. You can put whatever publisher imprint you like on the title page, but as far as stores, libraries, and even the Amazon website are concerned, the publisher is the cringe-worthy *Independently published*. If I were starting new today, I would certainly buy for the package of one hundred from Bowker. I'm sorry I took those freebies! As more and more would-be authors discovered how easy and cheap it is to have their names in print, the Amazon labels became a warning flag. (Do a search on Amazon Books for **"Independently published"** — including the quotation marks. Is that the company you want your book to keep?)

And the Amazon connection probably kills your chances of being stocked in a bricks-and-mortar bookstore, whose owners view Jeff Bezos as the beast that ate the book business. Fortunately, that thinking hasn't yet affected the online bookstores. If you opt for Expanded Distribution, B&N, Books-a-Million, the Book Depository, and others will sell your books online.

As a US publisher buying your ISBNs, you should set up an account at **MyIdentifiers.Com**. Then go to **My Account > Manage ISBNs**, where you can upload the cover, enter the "metadata" for your book, and — if you are distributing through IngramSpark — specify your terms for supplying copies to retailers. (Booksellers expect a discount of at least 40 percent and will be happier with 50 percent. They also expect to be able to return books that don't sell.) All this becomes a part of your book's entry in *Books in Print*, so it can be ordered online by any bookstore worthy of the name.

The LCCN

Another number? Yes, if you hope to be cataloged by an American library, you should get a Library of Congress Control Number, *before* you publish your book. Go to **LOC.Gov/publish/pcn** and click on the *PrePub Book*

Link. (If you signed up for the LCCN program earlier, be aware that accounts did not migrate to the new platform. You must sign up again.) Next, click on *Request LCCN* and begin the process, first entering your book's information, then the author's, then the title page details (you can upload a PDF of the actual page instead, and note that you must supply a US city where the publisher is located), and so on through the system..

With the LCCN number, you have a chance of being accepted into the Library of Congress catalog. (Nonfiction has an edge, since the LOC favors subjects like local history that aren't covered by traditional publishers.) You must submit two copies of the printed book. If accepted, it will be fully cataloged, providing you with a "data block" you can add to your copyright page and enables any library anywhere in the US to add your book to its catalog.

Designing Your Book

I trust you have acquired *The Chicago Manual of Style*, as advised in the previous chapter. It's a university-level course in the theory, design, and editing of books, and it's especially important for your paperback. If you don't have it, do yourself a favor: buy the book, study it, and refer to it often. (A secondhand copy will do, because the changes tend to be minute. The 17th edition, for example, okays the use of "US" rather than the traditional "U.S." with two full stops.)

My own workflow is so idiosyncratic that I describe it only as an illustration of what's possible. I compose almost everything in WordStar, a program I discovered in 1982 when I bought an Olympia electronic typewriter with a gorgeous keyboard and a computer extension that sat off to the side. It looked a bit like a big-headed alien.

The text was orange, on a black background. "Hard to learn, easy to use," went the software mantra in the 1980s; "easy to learn, hard to use." WordStar came with a training manual that took me two weeks to master. (Today, if I can't have a software up and running in fifteen minutes, I generally abandon it as a bad job.) But oh, once mastered, what glorious ease in writing, editing, and revising! Those WordStar keyboard commands are so embedded in my fingers that to compose or edit in a conventional software like Microsoft Word is like seeing the world through a straw. (Happily, I have a set of keyboard commands written by Mike Petrie that bring some but not all of WordStar's genius to Word.)

Nevertheless, my books do end up as Word docs, and it's then that I start preparing them for publication. This is how:

Smarten it up

Like the Army-surplus Remington upon which I learned to touch-type with one of my buddies and twenty girls from our high school's Secretarial curriculum, WordStar didn't provide curly quotes or proper em dashes. So the first thing I do after opening my book file in Word is to do a search and replace for double quotes, then for single quotes and dashes Word does a brilliant job of inserting the curly quotes, single or double, right-facing or left-facing. The only place it falls down is with a truncated word like 'twas. The mark should curl to the right, but Word invariably supplies a left-facing one. You'll probably know if you have any truncated words in your book.

Finally, I replace all instances of a double hyphen with Word's shortcut for an em dash, which is ^+.

But I trust you won't have to do any of that. There are a few WordStar writers still publishing, but not many.

Cut it down to size

KDP Print allows you to upload a Word doc to its website. Please don't do this! Automagical conversions are almost never satisfactory. What psychologists call "confirmation bias" may persuade you that the result is handsome, but trust me on this — it isn't. You can also find templates online that claim to make the formatting easy. I don't particularly like templates, either, though they're certainly safer than throwing a Word doc against the wall and hoping it will dry and fall off as a book. But I prefer to do the formatting myself, just as I do with e-books.

However you go about it, you must first decide on the dimensions of your page. I like 5.5x8.5 inches unless the book runs to 300 pages or more, in which case I would go with 6x9 inches, giving me a larger canvas to work on. Print-on-demand is possible only because of a process called "perfect binding." The machine clamps the pages together, trims them to the finished size, applies glue to the spine, and presses the paper cover into place. If a book has, say, 500 pages, the reader must open it almost flat, and may actually break it in half. You've probably done this to old mass-market paperbacks.

Both 5.5x8.5 and 6x9 are industry standards, hence economical to print, store, and ship. I apologize to the rest of the world for using what Americans still call "English measure." My two favored sizes come out to 216x140 mm and 229x152 mm.

I don't think it makes much sense to go smaller than 5.5x8.5. That's approaching the size of mass-market paperbacks with their dramatically lower prices, even as your minimum price increases because you will need more pages in the book. At Amazon, each page costs 1.2 cents, or 2.4 cents per sheet of paper.

Once you know the dimensions of the finished book, you can start to design it in your favorite word processor. As always when setting out on a new project, keep a backup copy of the original in case anything goes wrong. In my venerable version of Word (2007), the setup is hidden in plain sight. I go to the *Page Layout* screen and find *Page Setup,* on the bottom menu toward the left of the screen. It is evoked by clicking on a tiny box at the right. This brings up a window where I specify the margins, paper size, and layout of my book. If you are using OpenOffice or LibreOffice, your task is simplified, since by choosing *Format > Page* you can set all the parameters of your book.

Margins: Let's assume a book in the golden range of 150-300 pages. Much smaller, and the spine will be too narrow to display the title, author, and maybe a publisher's colophon (symbol). In that case, you might want to increase the number of pages by using a smaller trim size, a larger typeface, or more spacing between lines; by adding illustrations or background material; or by using both a header and a footer.

If your book is larger than 300 pages, you should consider a wider margin at the *gutter* — the inside edge, toward the spine. All my books have a top and bottom margin of 0.5 inch. If the book is skinny, I might use an outside margin of 0.6 inch; otherwise, 0.5 inch. At the gutter, I have used 0.9 inch for all but one of my books. The exception contains 358 pages, including the unnumbered pages at the front. This is not excessive in a conventionally bound book, which will more easily lie flat. But because of the "perfect binding" problem mentioned above, I allowed a gutter of 1.0 inch, which worked out fine. (Ignore Amazon's apparent recommendations for the margins. They are actually refer the absolute minimums, and you would be wise not to go there.)

Also in this window, select the *Orientation* of your page, which in almost every case will be *Portrait* (vertical). Finally, under *Pages > Multiple pages*, choose the option for *Mirror margins*. Now your verso (left-hand, even-numbered) pages will have the gutter on the right, while the recto (odd-numbered) pages have it on the left.

Paper: Yes, it's odd to set the margins before the page size, but I am just following the logic of Word's *Page Setup* window. The second option is *Paper*, and it suffices to set the *Width* and the *Height*. When you type the numbers, the window at the top will change to *Custom size*.

Layout: I do nothing here, because from this point forward I format my book in OpenOffice Writer. It's a workflow I developed when I was using an even older version of Word. I continue to use it because I find the Open Office menus more intuitive, because Word has an unfortunate habit of coarsening illustrations when saving them in the Personal Document Format (PDF), and because the PDF sometimes differed from the layout I had so painstakingly created. So I don't trust Word for this final — and to me crucial — step in the publishing process.

If you don't have Word, you must do all the above in OpenOffice Writer or its near twin, LibreOffice. The language will be slightly different, but you should have no problem figuring it out.

Design your book

When I open my Word doc in OpenOffice Writer, I am already ahead of the game, because OOW already shows me the mirrored pages, with even numbers on the left, odd numbers on the right, just as they will appear in the finished book. From here, there are multiple ways to proceed. What I describe below is a quick-and-dirty system, perfectly adequate for your first outing. Once you've found your favorite book design, you can save it as a *Custom Style*.

At the risk of repeating myself, you should be working with a copy of your book, making regular use of the *Control-Z* command that undoes what you just did. And when it looks good — save it! At intervals, save a copy. And at somewhat longer intervals, save it under a different title, so if you lose your way, there will always be a way back without losing days of work.

My first step is to go *Control-A* to mark the entire text. Then, from the top menu, I choose **Format > Character > Font**. I can now set the *typeface* and its size in *points*. (For what it's worth, there are 72 points to an inch, but just take it on faith: 10 point type is small, 13 point type is large.) Be aware that there may be significant differences between typefaces. I have settled on **Georgia** as my favorite. It's handsome, easy to read, and, um, *large* for its size. By that last phrase, I mean that 11 point Georgia looks almost as big as 12 point anything else, so I can safely use it when I'm trying to cut down on the number of pages, while reverting to 12 point for shorter books. If you prefer a more traditional typeface, then **Garamond** may suit you. Here, as always, the internet is your friend. There are dozens of websites out there, discussing typefaces and their uses. My advice is to avoid Times New Roman and Arial (the first was intended for a narrow newspaper column, while the second is a bit, um, *antiseptic*) as well as any typeface that is in the least way exotic.

Next, I let my lines "breathe." If you look at almost any book from a mainstream publisher, you will notice that there's space between the lines, called *leading* (pronounced "ledding") because in the days of the Linotype machine, the lines of type were cast from molten lead, and the operator manually inserted thin strips between them to fill a short column or make an opening paragraph easier to read.

Just as 10 point type is too small for most uses, so is single-spaced text too tight. I go to **Format > Paragraph > Indents & Spacing**, where I set the spacing to "at least" 0.02 inch, which just happens to be the default in a Kindle e-book. If you like, you might go a bit more, and you might also add a bit of padding between paragraphs. For what it's worth, the print edition of this book uses 0.02 inch spacing but has nothing additional between paragraphs except where I needed to balance the length of facing pages..

I have tried these instructions on a LibreOffice file, and the language is almost exactly the same.

Headers, footers, front matter

I know it's very bad of me, but I have mostly given up the **header**, the traditional line across the top of most text pages, usually with the book title centered on the left-hand page and the chapter title centered on the right-hand page, with a page number on the outside. Instead, I settle for a **footer** with the page number centered. This avoids the problem of what to do on the first page of each chapter. Book designers like to keep such pages clean of distractions, as you can see by looking at any book from a reputable publisher. A page number at the bottom, by contrast, looks perfectly fine. Similarly, I don't number the first several pages. The tradition calls for lower-case roman numerals on some but not all of these pages. I urge you to read the **front matter** chapter in the *Chicago Manual*, so you'll know how it's meant to be done; then you can choose to follow tradition or my minimalist approach or something between. For me, the front matter contains six pages:

* The first recto page is the *half-title* or bastard title, with the book title in capital letters, perhaps in 14-point type, centered, toward the top.

* Overleaf is the first verso page, which may be blank or part of a two-page spread for the title. I use it to list my previously published books. Why not?

* The *title page* is next. I spend some time on designing this, usually using italics for the title and subtitle, sometimes putting the title in capital letters, and incorporating my colophon or publisher's logo. When it's done, I take a screenshot that I will use in the digital edition of the book.

* The *copyright page* is on the back of the title page. (A Big Five publisher would number this page iv.) If I have a dedication or epigraph or other such material, I generally put it above the copyright statement.

* The *Table of Contents* is the next recto page (and might be numbered v).

* The sixth front matter page may be blank, display a *frontispiece* or an *epigram*, or continue the table of contents (in which case it might be numbered vi).

Today, fewer books pad out the front matter with a preface (written by the author) or foreword (written by someone else) or other throat-clearing material, but you certainly can if you like. I prefer to work this material into the text, or I put it at the back of the book.

Pagination

Here we have what I find to be the toughest part of formatting the print edition: putting the Arabic numeral *1* on a page that is actually the seventh page of the book. Though I am happy to do without headers, and without roman numerals in the front matter, I am bothered to see a number 7 on the first page of text. (For reasons of my own, I did just that with the print edition of this Guide. I wanted to refer back to the frontispiece, so I put the numeral 2 on it, and of course that the seventh page had to be numbered 7.)

Here again, the internet is our friend. There's a somewhat baffling tutorial on the **Apache OpenOffice User Guide** that I printed out and refer to, each time I need unpaginated front matter. The crucial steps are these:

* Make an empty paragraph at the end of your final front matter page, which will be a verso page and may or may not have text on it.

* Put your mouse cursor on the new blank line.

* **Choose Insert > Manual Break.**

* Select **Page break** and choose the **Default** style.

* Select the **Change page number** check box and set the new value to Arabic numeral 1. Click OK to close the dialog box.

That seems very straightforward, but for some reason it isn't, and I don't find the process in Word any easier. Search the internet until you find something that makes sense to you. There are even YouTube tutorials for those who find it easier to follow a video than words on a screen.

There's also a brute-force workaround that has been recommended to me. If you have Adobe Acrobat or similar software, you can build one PDF for the front matter and a second for the rest of the book – then combine them. And note that the Draft2Digital conversion mentioned elsewhere avoids the pagination problem altogether.

Drop caps

Yes, I want drop-caps in the print edition, though I shy away from them in my e-books. Usually I limit them to the first line in a chapter, along with a few words in upper case (all caps). This is easily done in OpenOffice Writer: **Format > Paragraph > Drop Caps**. Click on **Display drop caps**. The default is a single character over three lines, with no extra space between it and those lines. That's probably what you want, though not always. A couple years ago I formatted a lengthy book, with lengthy chapters, so I used two-line drop caps to introduce major sections within each chapter. And yes, I some-times used a drop cap even when it wasn't strictly necessary, just to relieve the monotony of multiple pages of text.

Special situations? If a chapter begins with a quotation, you might need two characters in the drop cap, with the first being the quotation mark. (Or omit the mark, if you prefer.) And you will find that if your first paragraph has fewer than three lines, you can't have a three-line drop cap. In such a case, I would do a bit of rewriting.

And there are two situations where you might want to increase the space between the drop cap and the next letter. If your first word is a single letter — *I* and *A* being the most likely candidates — you should add enough space to make that obvious. And some letters, in some typefaces, may seem to crowd the next letter, and a hair-line space will improve the appearance.

Hyphens, widows, orphans

Right about here, the author-publisher begins to understand why there is such a profession as book designer. We have volunteered to do every job — editing, proofreading, and now formatting — so it behooves us to be as professional as we can. On the self-publishing forums, I often see posts from authors who claim they can format a book in fifteen minutes. What they're really saying is that they throw sixty thousand words at a website and trust to luck. Personally, I often spend a week smoothing the layout of the print edition, though taking frequent breaks to work on something less fussy.

After the drop caps are settled, I tackle word spacing, line by line. Auto-hyphenation has been getting better, as witness Kindle books that have "enhanced typesetting" which, thanks to Kindle Format Ten (KFX), improves the appearance of e-books on newer devices and apps. I am impressed by the results, but I don't think they're good enough for a print edition. E-books are more ephemeral than print editions: we don't *own* them, really, so much as license, borrow, or steal them. It's the difference between owning a CD and having the song on an iPod.

I go through each chapter line by line, entering a manual hyphen wherever there's too much white space in a line. I regularly enter the candidates at the Hyphenation24 website, which is almost as good as Mrs. Zulauf, my twelfth-grade English teacher. (Though not as good, I'm afraid, as the rules in the *Chicago Manual of Style*, which you ought to read before starting this task.) Be aware that hyphenating one word in a paragraph will change the spacing in the following line, perhaps requiring another hyphenation or even getting rid of the first hyphen as the lesser evil. I try to avoid more than two end-of-line hyphens in a row.

There's a rule against hyphenating a word so that some syllables appear on one page and the rest on the next, but I violate this rule if I have to. Similarly, there's a rule against widows (the last line of a paragraph at the top of a page) and orphans (the first line of a paragraph at the bottom of a page). To me, the second seems a small offense, and even the first is acceptable if the line is reasonably full. Otherwise some discreet editing is called for, and it is here that you have an advantage over the professional, because you don't have to email the author to get permission! Similarly, I sometimes go back and revise a paragraph or two in order to get rid of a lonely few lines on the last page of a chapter.

We don't have software as powerful as that available to a book designer at Doubleday or Penguin, but we do have a few tools to smooth out a page. The first is *tracking* — adding a tiny space between characters in order to spread them more generously across the page. (It's also possible, if less common, to subtract a sliver.) Think of tracking as a more precise tool than hyphenation. In OpenOffice Writer, mark the line with your cursor and go to **Format > Character > Position** and skip down to *Spacing*. The adjustment is by "points," but you can refine that by calling for 0.3 or 0.5 points. (Tracking is often confused with *kerning*, which refers to adjusting the space between two letters, such as AW, that because of their shape might seem widely spaced.)

While I might *expand* the characters on two or three lines on a page, I don't think I have *condensed* characters on more than four lines in this entire book.

Similarly, we can adjust the length of a page by using **Format > Paragraph > Indents & Spacing** to increase or decrease the space between lines or paragraphs. I sometimes do this to ensure that facing pages come out to the same length, for example when a subhead throws off the spacing.

From Design to Print

You can of course do all the design work in Microsoft Word, though not as easily in my opinion. But now you should save your book in Personal Document Format for uploading to KDP Print, and this is another task where the competition shines. Early versions of Word did a miserable job of outputting PDFs, and most versions have the additional disadvantage that they save images at a resolution of 200 dots per inch (dpi). That's too low-rez for the print edition. OpenOffice and LibreOffice, by contrast, will preserve any resolution that your photo-editing software can produce. POD printers recommend, and I strive for, at least 300 dpi. KDP Print is notorious for rejecting any book that fails this hurdle, whereas CreateSpace merely threw up a warning, while allowing you to proceed if you insisted.

Just choose **File > Export as PDF** and and check that images are at 100 percent quality or 300 dots per inch, and that the output is **PDF/A-1a**. The software will create a file with the same name as your book file, with a *.pdf* extension.

It's here that I do my almost-final proofing. You can of course do this in your word processor, but some pub-lishers have reported that making a PDF can alter the layout, perhaps pushing a word to the next page and thereby creating an orphan, which can throw off every page that follows. I've never seen this — perhaps it only happens with Word. In any case, I print two copies of the PDF. I take one copy, give the other to Susan, and spend several days — probably a week — reading the whole thing aloud to her. (It's not a full-time job. We'll read a chapter an hour, one in the morning and a second in the afternoon, so we don't get stale.) Luckily for me, she was an editor in an earlier life, she too had a good English teacher in high school, and she has more or less mem-orized *The Elements of Style* and *The Chicago Manual of Style*.

Mind you, we're not *editing* the book at this stage.

We're looking for gross errors. When I tweak things, I inevitably make a mistake (or two, or three), so at this point I do as little tweaking as possible.

Then it's back to the word processor to make the corrections and export the final PDF for uploading to KDP Print (and perhaps to Ingram Spark).

The KDP Publishing Process

I'm assuming you have already set up a KDP account. If you are starting with the paperback edition, click on that option under **Create a New Title** at the top of the screen. If you have already published or started the Kindle edition, click on **Create Paperback** in the Bookshelf listing for your book. Either way, this brings up a set of three tabs very like those for publishing an e-book, and if you have already worked on the e-book, many of the fields will already be populated. As with the Kindle edition, be strict about capitalization. As you might expect in this internet age, there's even a website called **Capitalize My Title** that will do the job for you. It's very good — just start typing. I click on the *Chicago* option, shorthand for the eponymous *Manual of Style*; the others are a bit too relaxed for book publishing.

A crucial point: before you click on **Save & Continue**, go back and check your title, because no change can be made in it after the ISBN has been assigned.

The ISBN

The next tab deals with the book's content, and it starts with the ISBN. If you choose the "free" one from Amazon, the software will churn a bit and produce a 13-digit number such as 9781539309154. Properly hyphenated, it's actually *978-1-5393-0915-4*, which translates as:

978: The prefix (979 is another option now in use).

1: The language is English.

5393: The publisher was Amazon's now-defunct CreateSpace division.

0915: This was number 915 in that particular Create-Space series.

4: And this was the "checksum," which validates the other numbers.

There is also a 10-digit ISBN, *1539309150*, omitting the prefix and with a different checksum, but otherwise containing the same information. The KDP platform won't display this number, but it will appear on the Amazon store, along with the 13-digit version, and is often used when linking to the book. (In both cases, those are the ISBNs of the print edition of this Guide.)

If instead you choose to provide your own ISBN, you are given two windows, one to insert the 13-digit number, the other to insert your imprint or publisher name. This must conform exactly to the information you entered at MyIdentifiers dot com, as described above.

Note that the full ISBN must appear on the copyright page of your book, so if you intend to take Amazon's "free" number, you should begin the publishing process before finishing the PDF.

The physical book

Next there is a window for the publication date, which I suggest you leave blank, so the day it goes live on the Amazon store will be regarded as the day of publication. This is followed by **Print Options**. Color is very expensive in the POD process, so do not choose that option unless you are very sure that people will pay a high price for your book. I like cream paper for most purposes, and it's a bit thicker than white, which can bulk up a short book.

The default print size is 6x9 inches, but think twice before accepting it. It is simply not true, as Amazon will tell you, that most books are published this size. If you check the trade paperbacks on your bookshelf, I suspect you will find they are a bit smaller. Personally, I prefer 5.5x8.5 inches, which is closer to the size of the average trade paperback (and the average hardcover as well, if you ignore its covers). If you go much narrower than 5.5 inches, you may run into problems with the binding as mentioned above.

All my books have been no-bleed, meaning that no images are carried out to the outside edge. I have often expanded photos a bit, so that they spread outside the text border, but never as close as 0.25 inch inside the trim line. KDP Print is tricky when it comes to images that bleed, so avoid this option if you possibly can.

Your final choice is whether to use "matte" or glossy finish to your cover. I rather like matte, but it does show fingerprints more than the glossy covers, and it tends to soften the colors. Glossy is therefore probably the better choice, especially if you hope that your paperback will ever be stocked in a bricks-and-mortar store.

When it comes to uploading your book to the KDP platform, I hope you have created a print-ready and cleanly proofed PDF. If instead you choose to throw a word-processing document at the system, you will in my opinion richly deserve the likely consequences. By the same token, I hope you have a professionally designed cover. The KDP Print Cover Creator is very good, and I have sometimes designed a front cover (including 0.125 inch trim on the three outside edges) on Canva.com, then used the KDP wizard to build the back cover and the spine. Building a wraparound cover is beyond my skill level; if you want to attempt it, you can get a right-sized template from Bookow.com.

A Way Around All That

While window shopping at the *Kboards Writers Cafe* — an excellent source of information and inspiration — I found another way to get a paperback into print, and that's through **Draft2Digital**, the same aggregator I use to sell e-books outside the Amazon mini-verse. I don't find it entirely satisfactory, because I regard my books as purchases for the long haul, deserving of a place on the owner's bookshelf. But if you are a writer of what I might call *disposable* fiction, you probably won't sell many paperbacks, and those are likely to go to readers with a forgiving disposition: they just want to be entertained for a few hours. Meanwhile, your e-book will benefit from the added credibility (and apparent price discount) made possible by the existence of a print edition.

Simply upload a well-formatted Word doc to the D2D platform — and it *must* be well formatted, using heading and text styles and a Word-generated table of contents. Select from among a menu of themes, and presto! You are given a PDF file with the text properly paginated, justified, and hyphenated. If you don't want to spend days and weeks perfecting your book, you might give it a try. D2D will handle the distribution, or you can take the PDF and market it through IngramSpark or Amazon.

I have also mentioned **Kindle Create**, Amazon's software for formatting e-books. It will similarly produce a print edition of sorts, so if you have reconciled yourself to KC's disadvantages, you might also be satisfied with its print output.

Finishing Up

The final tab deals with pricing, the Expanded Distribution option, and lastly the chance to get a physical proof copy of your book. I urge you to skip to the bottom and order that proof before you do anything else, and certainly before you click on *Publish Your Paperback Book*. The cost including shipping is typically $7-$8, and no money in publishing is better spent. I think you should spend several days closeted with the book, and if you find errors or omissions, fix them, and perhaps order another proof to make sure everything is right. You simply cannot be too hasty here.

Pricing. Self-publishers tend to undervalue their print editions. Give yourself a decent profit! The money you receive isn't really a royalty, as Amazon presents it. Instead, it is your *gross revenue* as the book's publisher, which must cover all the cost of building and marketing the book before any royalty is paid to you as the author. (This becomes more clear if you opt for Expanded Distribution and see how much revenue disappears when other distributors take their cut.) As with the e-book, the US dollar price is the base, and you can simply let the other Amazon stores convert from there. I don't think you should do this. For this book, I charge $10.95 on the US store, £8.95 for the British edition, €9.95 for the other European stores, and 1295 yen for Japan. It's important not to underprice for Japan, where the yen is worth less than one US cent, because if the price is set too low the software won't let you publish.

Expanded Distribution. I am a strong believer in this option, which CreateSpace long offered and which KDP Print finally adopted. I price my books so that they return a minimum royalty of $1.50 when sold outside the Amazon mini-verse — and "outside" actually includes several Amazon stores, including India and China, as well as such online bookstores as Barnes & Noble and the Book Depository. Because the intermediate distributors take their cut, the total bookseller share increases from 40 percent in the case of direct Amazon sales to 60 percent. So your final price must allow for that, plus the cost of printing the book, and of course for your own profit. In the case of this Guide, with a retail price of $10.95 and printing cost of $2.60, I earn $3.97 from a sale on the US Amazon store and $1.61 from one on Barnes & Noble. (Your revenue elsewhere will be higher if you distribute through IngramSpark instead of using Amazon's Expanded Distribution option. And note that B&N Press also gets your book onto British websites like Waterstones.)

While a KDP paperback goes live on the Amazon stores in one day or less, those to the "expanded" outlets will take a month or more.

Goodbye and Good Luck!

When I find myself writing about the ins and outs of print editions, I have left my area of expertise. (I have never distributed a book through IngramSpark or Barnes & Noble, and I didn't use KDP Print until I was forcibly moved over.) Besides, I think I've made my approach clear enough in the course of this Guide: Write your book, format it well, make it available in every country and on every retailer you possibly can, market it industriously — then write another book and do the same with that.

There is no secret formula. Writers succeed in self-publishing just as they do in traditional publishing, because people like to read their books, and because they've had a bit of luck. I would like to think that only the good writers succeed, and then only if their books are well-formatted, with professionally designed covers, but alas that isn't true. I spend a lot of time on the Kindle Community forums, and sometimes it is the poster who can't write or punctuate on the level I'd expect of a high school sophomore who turns out to have a book ranking at a very respectable 2,500 (meaning that 2,499 books sell better than his or hers, according to the mysterious algorithm that Amazon uses to measure popularity). No one has ever figured out how this works. Just do your best, write a lot, and don't blame Jeff Bezos or me if you are languishing down there with a sales ranking of 500,000 or even 1,000,000. All of us have been there at one time or another, either on the way up or on the way down. Enjoy the trip! — *NJ Notjohn, August 2020*

Printed in Great Britain
by Amazon